PASSIONABILITY

Igniting a Life Full of Love, Happiness, and Meaning

Randa El Zein

Be You International

Randa El Zein
Be You International
Office #701, NBK building
Abu Dhabi, United Arab Emirates
info@beyouinternational.com
www.BeYouInternational.com

ISBN 978-9948-39-700-7

Approved by the National Media Council -MC-02-01-9964667

Limits of Liability and Disclaimer of Warranty

Cover design by Kojic Zeljka

Typesetting services by BOOKOW.COM

For my dad.
His constant love, endless support,
and words of encouragement
made this book possible.

Kind words from private coaching clients

"I still remember when Randa asked me in the first session: do you love yourself? I paused, didn't know what to answer as I never thought about it. She taught me to love myself, to turn every bad experience into a learning one, to be more in control. I'm more outgoing, self-expressive, socializing more, doing stuff out of my comfort zone, understanding myself more, loving myself more. The effect has been more on letting the change cross over to my job in terms of self-confidence, public speaking and taking decisions. We meet lots of people in our life. Some you might forget their names and some you never will. Randa, I will always remember your smile and positive words. Big thank you for you, and for Be You." - Lina Hajar, Abu Dhabi

"Since the beginning of my coaching classes I have been thinking to myself 'what will this do for me?' and 'how and when will I see the benefits from this coach?' Randa was not a therapist, nor was she someone who told me what to do. She was a coach. Someone who encouraged me, pushed me, helping me to see the ideas I was trying to create. A coach who helped me put my ideas into action and let me drive those actions into the results I so desperately wanted to achieve. Randa used great models and exercises along with challenges to get me to my goals. As these tools were taught and experienced, I started seeing results right away in my work life, home life and also play. I have grown into a better leader at work, a husband and father at home and have now been able to design and enjoy my free time the way I wanted with all three quadrants of my life meshing well with each other. I recommend this to all people regardless of the task, roadblock or confusion one may have in their own life. My advice is to trust the process and use the techniques she may offer. A giant thanks to Randa El Zein from me, my family, friends and co-workers." - Anthony Haack

"Randa is a ball of positivity. Her dynamic approach enables women to change perspective and realize that they can achieve what their heart desires." - Inez Moutarde, Switzerland

"Randa's ability to connect with her client, regardless of their age, sex and background, is a talent and gift seldom found in people and rarely utilized constructively. As someone who was always nicknamed Doubting Thomas, Randa treaded lightly over my fears and hesitation until they were all dismissed. I am not a person who reads self-help books, but conversing with a woman whose passion is to help is an experience I strongly recommend to everyone who's about to 'settle' and accept things as they are." -Abdallah Al Shami; Special Projects Editor for Shawati', Abu Dhabi, UAE.

"I came to Randa stuck and overwhelmed. She helped me clarify and set goals based on my values. More importantly, her Passion Test really helped me to apply a value-based lens to all of my decision making! The time spent with Randa was fun, relaxed, extremely informative, and very productive. Asking for Randa's help is one of the best things I've ever done for myself and if you are feeling stuck I would recommend you do the same." - Victoria Mironova, UAE

"Randa is sincere in her desire to help people achieve their goals and dreams. Having found what she is passionate about in life, she wants to help others learn how to be better and unleash their potential to live fulfilling lives." - S. Dvorancic; Commercial Realtor, Florida, USA

"Randa is an amazing life coach and close friend to her clients. I call her always the happiness butterfly:) because of the happiness dosage that she gave kindly to me every time I meet her. My experience with Randa was great since I met her for the first time in Happyness 101 and throughout the passion test, the coaching sessions and all the events she does. Randa helped me to know myself better and to know what's my passion in this life. I owe her a lot in changing my vision of life in many areas." - Fatin Bandora

"Randa helped me understand what positivity means. She taught me how to do everything in life out of love, be it for myself or for others. Coaching sessions are not meant to solve your problems but give you the right tools to do so. I believe Randa has made a difference doing this." - Hadeel Kassab

"I worked with Randa as a life coach back in 2012 and recommend her highly. She guided me through a process that was so effective in crystalizing some of my life goals so that their importance to me was immensely clear. Since that time, my steps have lead me ever closer to realizing those goals ... two of the very top ones have already been manifested in my life and I am grateful to Randa for leading me to those insights." - Michael Coady; Producer / Writer /Actor, Los Angeles, USA

"This Beyoutiful lady helped me feel whole again. Randa's questions provoked my passions to resurface, my insecurities to fade and my priorities to change for my betterment. I have never felt as empowered as I did leaving my first workshop with her, that weekend will be forever remembered. Be You is the brain Child of an amazingly talented, inspiring and empowering individual called Randa. She makes you question your insecurities, helps prioritise your passions and supports you in becoming the you, you want to be. If I could give more stars, I would loan some from the sky and happily award them to her." - Benash Nazmeen, UK

"Loved every minute of being coached. Now I honestly love the person I am today. We all need help at some point in our lives, and I am glad I listened to my gut and met up with Randa who totally changed my life for the better. She does amazing work, water for thirsty souls is the best description I can give, to be the best version of yourself! Two thumbs up for Randa!" - Mariam Janice, UAE

"Be You, led by Randa, is the engine of the pursuit of happiness, self-improvement, and betterment of the self. Through Randa's various classes, seminars and activities, there is vast potential to transfer the feel-good factor when attending, into actionable work items in order to achieve one's goals. One can choose to tackle several aspects of life which he/she wants to improve, and not only is the activity fun and engaging but is highly effective too!" - Paul Choufani, UAE

"Randa is an amazing life coach, she guides you to make the right choices in life, by always putting your happiness in the lead. She has taught me to look at my life and not to think of it as a huge mess, but embrace it and make the best out of it. Randa helped me set my priorities in life according to what I'm most passionate about, and that has eased my way through life. Thank you, Randa, for helping me realize what I should be focusing more on in my life!!" - Ola Khatib, UAE

"I can confidently say that I got more than my expectations, you made me realize emotional strengths deep rooted in me that I could not have found on my own and not only that but to put those strengths to use and see the results is far beyond anything I could say, really words are not enough to express how much I love you!" - Sahar, Abu Dhabi

"Randa is a passionate coach who is knowledgable and has many tools to work with. She can spot your limiting beliefs and help you break through them. She is strict yet loving and will hold you to a very high standard.

She will challenge you to push past your comfort zone. I have made great progress, and I'm excited to continue to work with her!" - SI, San Ramon, California

"I was trapped in my own mind looking at the world and wondering where am I going and why I couldn't live a fulfilling life. She was the first one to unlock me. Randa really helped me think through my emotions and needs. She taught me to identify each one of them and to live them fully in order to take the right measures and get results. The passion test is a revealing experience. It unfolded my subconscious to a surprisingly stunning 'picture.' I'm happier and freer than ever. And obviously, I now know where I am going. She promises you a life changing experience, and she delivers on her promise." - Khadijah, UAE

"Life coaching with Randa is a journey, one that she helps shape with my own hands. I first find out that I have built many walls in my mind. Some of these walls have been there since before I remember, and some are new. What lies on the other side of each wall, is a dream. I entertain several possibilities of what I might turn out to be: a banker, an economist, a chef, a musician, and a writer. Randa has armed me with the power of self-awareness and visualization; one to question the existence of the wall, and one to make what's on the other side tangible, visible, audible, even edible. When one would say to me, unleash your potential, it really wasn't immediately clear how I could do that. Randa shows me how to take down these walls and how to play an active role in the forming of new pillars of motivation and strength, and the strength is in the purpose. I believe she knows that the foundation most of us stand upon is weak, and based on living a passive life. Come with an open mind, leave with a new life." - Omar, Lebanon

"I have worked with Be You International for over a year now and in spite of my struggle for work/life balance Randa has been unwavering with a firm, but supportive guidance on redefining a mind, body and spirit lifestyle into a more healthful and productive plan. I am deeply grateful for the life line that Randa has provided in her commitment, positive energy, and inspiration." - D. Bregenzer, Business Consultant, USA

"My life was just all over the place - literally. I felt like the walls were closing in on me and I don't know where to begin to straighten it out let alone know how to do so. Contacting Randa was the best decision I did in a really long time. Randa taught me how to look at things from a different perspective. She showed me what my real passions are, what I really need to focus on in my life, how to give things a shot, and how it's ok to fail and most importantly how to be a better version of myself. Randa, to you I will always be grateful. I really advise life coaching to everybody especially to students - having it in school curriculums is a necessity. People need to know their real passions from a young age instead of wasting years figuring it out." - Hana Yazbak

"Working with Randa as my life coach really pushed me to deep levels; areas I didn't want to really face, but needed to. She made that journey much easier. She not only provides relatable examples, she is able to call you out in a way that is gentle yet tough. She opens doors and ideas to your soul. Randa's energy is wonderful and contagious!" - Jenn Bader, Canada

"Randa has had a tremendous impact and changed my way of thinking about what life 'is supposed to be.' I have the power to change what I don't like by simply having a different perspective. More important, Randa has prompted me to dream again and to live out these dreams with passion." - Filomena Gasparro, Toronto

"Randa is the embodiment of Servant Leadership - evident from the moment you start collaborating with her. Randa is at once, passionate, intelligent, funny, and appropriately fierce. She cares about your success, and through the Passion Test, I learned so much more about who I am, than simply doing a 'values' exercise. If you're seeking clarity around your life purpose, core values, and future opportunities, contact Randa, and you will not be disappointed." - Jeff Hendler, Canada

"After taking the passion test with Randa, I was able to gain focus on true intention for my life. Within days I could already see the benefits of this consciousness manifesting in my life and am truly grateful. Randa is passionate about people finding happiness and truth in their lives and living to their full intended potential." - Julie McCormick Jennen, Canada

Also by Randa El Zein

Be You card set

This small box contains some very big and powerful messages. Use them every time you feel like you need a little encouragement, a pick-me-up, some inspiration, or a kick in the butt. They only tell what you already know deep inside. Let them serve you when you are feeling lost, uninspired, or demotivated. Let the cards be that other voice reminding you to always Be Authentic, Be True and to, most importantly, Be You.

Parents can use these cards as a tool to start a conversation with their kids about sensitive or critical matters that might be happening or to get shy kids to learn to express. You can also try picking a card a day and choosing to live that day being what the card suggests you to be. Watch as your experience of the world changes day by day because you are now choosing in advance how you want to feel and who you want to be.

Visit www.beyouinternational.com or participating bookstores across UAE to buy your own set.

Contents

Introduction

THIS is a book about the happy journey we call life and how to live it with meaning. It's a book about the road trip we decide to take and the life that happens on that trip. The destination is almost irrelevant. It's how we go along that journey that determines our quality of life, our level of happiness, and how fulfilled we feel.

I smile as I am typing away, and I hope everyone reading this will be inspired to have the courage to start walking down the path their heart has chosen, a path usually less traveled and completely powered by passion. My wish is that it may even have you stop walking for a bit to take stock of the distance you've traveled so far, to reassess where you've been, where you are, and exactly where you're heading.

No matter where you are in life, you are one decision— one choice away—from a whole new beginning. You can act now, or you can wait and be stuck in an unfulfilling life. Just take care of step one, and all the rest of the steps will flow. The universe will provide and give you clues. Don't go with the flow; *be* the flow.

Whatever you do, I trust you're holding this book in your hands because it has called out to you. That's the way I buy my books. I'm sure you'll receive the lessons you're meant to or need at this point in your life through the pages to come.

My intention is to inspire younger people early on in their lives to realize their passions and live their lives aligned with those passions. I know I missed out on a couple of decades of living happily, and I am now determined to see that others won't have to if I can help it. Life is like a long corridor with many doors, and you can choose to open and go through any of them. My hope is that through this book, you'll have a master key that can open any door for you. With that kind of power, making choices becomes easy, but with choice comes responsibility. There are no mistakes, so whatever door you choose, it will be the perfect choice for you at that time.

I'm offering you an invitation to look at some new ways, tools, perspectives, and options on tackling life. I'll give you skills that will serve you now and that you can use in your everyday life—practical skills you can play with to get more out of every aspect of your life. Skills that will only work if you use them! That's the whole idea behind a self-help book. You have to help yourself. You are the one doing the work. The book is only a guide. The book is only giving you information, and that is pretty useless unless you put that knowledge into practice.

You have likely heard the saying "If I knew then what I know now." Well, I'll be sharing some stories from my own life experiences with you to illustrate what I know now and how not knowing something back then had an impact.

You can take the messages in this book and change them, tweak them, challenge them, and then choose to live them or not. This book is a compilation of almost everything I know and teach in my workshops and programs and in my private coaching practice as well. It contains knowledge I've acquired through the years from books that have transformed my life and my understanding of it; from courses and experiential learning events I've attended that have changed the course of my life; and from all sorts of studies, TED talks, documentaries, and research I've dug into online. I believe it's called stealing if you learn something and don't share it or teach it to others. This is my way of passing the torch.

Based on Edgar Dale's cone of experience that he laid out in 1940, we retain only a tiny percentage of what we read; we retain more of what we hear and even more of what we see. However, when we simultaneously hear and see, we retain considerably more of the material—even more still when we hear, see, and say—but we retain the biggest percentage of the material when we hear, see, say, and do. That's why I absolutely love giving and attending experiential learning workshops and retreats. You get to experience the lesson and therefore retain most of it in a fun environment. It took me six years to write this book. During that time, my work as a life coach evolved as I created workshops, programs, and retreats. In May 2018, I launched Passionability, an experiential learning event that I have put my heart and soul into.

The structure of this book follows the experience I took the participants through during the Passionability event. Just like a butterfly goes through three main stages of transformation, this book is divided into three parts. The first is about working hard to find out what type of person you are and getting down to the nitty-gritty of what it takes to find your passion and what brings meaning to your life.

In the second part, like a cocoon, we're going to go deep inside and understand our psychology; what controls our life; and why we act, react, and think the way we do.

The last part is about focusing on what would empower and enable us to live our passions and have a life of meaning —for without taking care of our wings, we cannot fly.

I initially wanted to call this book *The Little Happy Book* and make happiness its main focus. Then I changed my mind. While happiness should be sought for its own sake, every goal, dream, accomplishment, and material thing we want to acquire; the power we want to gain; the beauty we want to attain; or the money we want to earn is all because we expect these things will make us happy. But do they all necessarily make us so?

True happiness comes from being in the flow. Psychologist Mihaly Csikszentmihalyi said that happiness is a state of mind. He called it "the flow." And when we are immersed in the flow and doing something rewarding, something that fulfills all our needs on every level, then we are happy. Therefore, this book is about finding your passion and developing the ability to live your life aligned with that passion.

To get the most out of this book, you'll need:

1. A journal or notebook for writing down all your thoughts and notes or action steps so you can have them all together for future reference. This journal will, as is the case with some of my coaching clients, become your personal coach and best teacher.

2. A pen, a pencil, and highlighters. (Yes, you'll really want to make the book your own; lots of color is good!)

3. Thirty minutes a day for a week (give or take), though I'm secretly hoping that this will be the kind of book you feel you can't put down.

4. A friend to share with, to teach, and to hold you accountable. This is the best way to learn and to make sure you have grasped the lessons yourself.

The idea is not to keep the book looking the way it did when you first bought it. You may want to dog-ear some pages. You may find yourself marking them, highlighting sections that resonate with you, and adding your own notes, or taking out a whole page, framing it, and putting it up on your wall. Who knows? All of that is okay. It's your book. This is your journey, so make the most of it.

I suggest you first read through the book once. Then read it again—this time at a slower pace—and allow yourself time to digest the material as you do the suggested exercises. If you work through it progressively, by the time you finish, you'll already have put into action the domino effect that will change your life.

Part I

Caterpillars

In the infinity of life where I am, all is perfect, whole and complete and yet life is ever changing. There is no beginning and no end, only a constant cycling and recycling of substance and experiences. Life is never stuck or static or stale, for each moment is ever new and fresh. I am one with the very Power that created me, and this Power has given me the power to create my own circumstances. I rejoice in the knowledge that I have the power of my own mind to use in any way I choose. Every moment of life is a new beginning point as we move from the old. This moment is a new point of beginning for me right here and right now. All is well in my world.

—Louise L. Hay

Chapter 1

The Two Most Important Things in Life

There is no greater agony than bearing an untold story inside you.

—Maya Angelou

'M sure you've heard that happiness is a choice. That sounds simple enough. Why aren't more people choosing it? They say happiness is an inside job. Why aren't more people finding it?

The short answer is that what you focus on expands in your life, and you focus on your thoughts. They keep repeating in your head, and you manifest a life aligned with them. The long answer is what I'll be explaining to you in this book.

I remember it like it was yesterday. My mum had just bought me the reading books they required at school. I remember one book in particular. It was orange and had a picture of a little girl on the cover. The story started with "I walked and I walked." I clearly remember reading those words for the first time and pronouncing the silent *L* in *walked* incorrectly. I was no more than seven or eight years old.

For the longest time, I've had a strong urge to write a book on what I've learned about life so far. I didn't know what to write about exactly at the beginning, but a picture of a blank, open book is on one of my old vision boards, a subconscious message for me that the story is being written.

As I sat attempting to write this book, all sorts of thoughts went through my head. Thoughts like *Who do you think you are? Do you really think you can write a book? English isn't your first language; are you sure you want to do this? Why would anyone want to read it? If they did, would they like it? Can I really come up with a book that's as good as all the books I've fallen in love with, books that have changed my life? Will it measure up to any of the books I have sitting on my bedside table right now?*

The fear those thoughts created was enough to take me spiraling downward into a dark place—the kind of place where nothing happens. It's a place where I feel sorry for myself, a place where negativity reigns. I felt overwhelmed and inadequate as if I were taking on the mission of saving the world and doing it all in one day. I finally declared I was in an official panic attack. I started looking for other things I needed to do. All of a sudden, tidying up my closet and maybe painting the walls a new color became top priorities … anything to escape my thoughts and the task of writing this book. I even started looking for other people to blame for my fears because it's always easier to blame someone else for your problems.

Where do I go from here? I asked myself. One important thing I learned early on but really grasped and understood only recently is that I had a choice. I always have a choice, even when it doesn't look like there is one. It's all about claiming that power to choose that makes all the difference in one's life.

So, there I was, sitting all alone with my laptop in front of me. I stared at it as all my negative thoughts about my dream, my life, and myself float in the air around me. Luckily for me, the thought that was shouting the loudest was the one saying, "I have a choice."

I have a choice, I told myself. *I can pack up and forget about this whole idea. I'll feel a little sad because I've given up on something I really want to do, but I'd also feel okay because it is the easy way out, because it doesn't require me to change or get out of my comfort zone or risk rejection. Or I can start typing and see what happens.*

You know, waiting for courage to come so you can act on something is a form of procrastination. Waiting for all the negative thoughts in my head to go away would have been a good excuse not to do anything. If I just started typing, I'd have nothing to lose. Moreover, I'd feel like I'd accomplished something very important in my life. It could boost my career as a life coach. It could enable me to share the many things I want to put out there in the world for people to take and be inspired by, to compel them into action to change their lives and get out of their comfort zones. It could be the beginning of something really good. And, most important, if I went ahead and did this, I wouldn't end up spending the rest of my life asking the question, "How different would everything in my life be if I had just written that book?"

I made my choice ... and I started typing. This book in your hands is the result of the many hours, days, months, and years I've lovingly put into it. Doubt and negativity stopped me many times, even toward the end, after having written almost two hundred pages, but I persevered.

Inner peace is something we all want. To have a stress-free, calm, and relaxed mind is what we'd all like to have. When we have that, we're most resourceful, productive, and creative. But then a thought, or a whole bunch of thoughts, barge in, interrupting that peaceful state of mind. It becomes, instead, a monkey mind. I taught this concept to a group of sixty officials from provincial, national, and local government entities across the United Arab Emirates (UAE). At the very moment I was speaking about the mind wanting to achieve a peaceful state, I'd arranged to have boxes of cupcakes with sparkles and smiley faces brought into the room and served individually, with a bit of a staged racket. Everyone's attention moved from me to the cupcakes. Yes, they were all adults in the room, and the cupcakes became more important than me!

This is the perfect moment to tell you about my Vipassana retreat that I took in Ras Al Khaimah, UAE. It was a ten-day silent meditation retreat during which we meditated for ten hours every day, starting before sunrise. It was and still is, the most difficult thing I've ever done in my life.

It was truly silent. Even at meal times and during the little breaks we had, there was no talking and no eye contact because they are also forms of communication. Every morning, I saw the amazing sunrise and found myself frantically looking for my phone to take a picture, but we had had to surrender all our electronics at registration. I wanted to tell somebody to look but couldn't because we were in silence. Why couldn't I just enjoy the view for myself and appreciate that it was mine to savor quietly without the urge to share?

It took me three whole days of trying before I managed a full minute—not an hour or a day, but one single full minute—of proper meditation, when no thoughts got in the way and all I was doing was following the simple instruction of breathing in and out. That was when I met my mind face-to-face for the first time in my life. And I realized how crazy that is.

The mind keeps repeating stories all the time. It's a non-stop thought-making machine. The very first time I was introduced to meditation, I thought I would die if I tried to just sit and breathe for five whole minutes without thinking of anything as suggested. "Oh, that's so difficult," I said. "I can't do that because my mind won't stop thinking." But try I did. Now I can easily meditate for an hour; thoughts flow in, and I gently shoo them away and continue breathing in and out.

This is the most important thing I'm going to say in this book, so bust out your highlighters. Every single moment of every day, whether you're aware of it or not, you're doing one thing consistently: thinking!

More specifically, you're choosing your thoughts. In other words, every single moment, you're choosing what you want to focus on. You give that focus a meaning, which creates an emotion inside you. Then you decide what you'll do accordingly. When you act on something, you've made a decision. Every action you choose to take is initiated by a decision. So, it's not your conditions that shape your life; it's your decisions and choices.

When the cupcake boxes entered the room, those sixty officials could have chosen to keep focusing on the presentation or on what was in those boxes. Thoughts started to storm through their minds. *Are they going to reach me? Oh my God, I'm sitting at this far table; maybe there won't be enough by the time they get here. What's in those boxes anyway? Whatever it is, I want one, even if I don't!*

> *Obstacles are those frightful things you see when you take your eyes off your goal.*
>
> —Henry Ford

So, what should you focus your mind on? Thought you'd never ask. There are two very important things to focus on in life:

1. The goals and needs that help you live your dreams. It's having your life aligned with your own belief system—most importantly, your belief in yourself. Your belief that you can make it, you can achieve it, you can do whatever you set your mind on doing. Your belief that you can live a life worth living. A life you've chosen for yourself. A life that makes you happy and fulfilled by honoring you being you.

2. Enjoying the journey along the path to living your dreams, achieving your goals, and meeting your needs. I'll be going deeper into those needs in the second part of the book. It's said that being happy is being wise. Only the wise manage to enjoy the journey. Here we're talking about experiencing an authentic state of sustained happiness not only for today or tomorrow but for the rest of your life. We're talking about a life of well-being in every sense of the word.

For example, my goal might be that I want to lose weight. Then I expect my partner to exercise with me so we can become accountability buddies. But let's say he's not interested in doing that. Do I become stressed about the whole thing? Do I get angry with my partner or even forget my idea of exercising to lose weight just because I don't want to do it alone? The journey—how I make my decisions, how I conduct myself, and how I treat others—is as important as the goal.

So *how* I'm trying to do what I want to do is the key to how happy my life is going to be, regardless of whether I reach my goal. How many people do you know who want to get to the top, want to go to the next level, want the next big thing, want the upgraded version of whatever it is, only to discover that when they reach the top or buy all those things, they still aren't happy? That's because they're missing the second important thing on which they need to focus: the how. We won't be there to listen to our own eulogy, but in every moment of our every living day, we're writing it. Our eulogy is all about *how* we lived.

A party without cake is just a meeting.

—Julia Child

Life without happiness is just a chore. Let's assume you're a pastry chef or a baker; making cakes is all you do. There's a fine balance between baking a cake, being a master at it, and eating it. How do you live your life? Are you so busy perfecting the art of baking cakes that you don't have time to enjoy them? Or do you spend most of your time experimenting with all sorts of cakes and laughing at yourself when you make a mistake? Do you end up enjoying those cakes you've baked? Do you share them with others and like baking for them? Here's another thought: Do you bake only when you have company and never allow yourself to indulge in eating cake solo? Do you take people's criticisms of your cakes lightly or become offended by them? Or do you leverage them as possibilities for improving your skill? Do you go all out because life is just better with butter, or do you calculate how many calories you're consuming with every bite of that cake? Do you cut the cake into pieces and always offer the bigger ones to others?

What we do in life and how we do it are two completely different things. You can have the noblest of intentions, but how you go about seeing them through could be so bad, constricting, or anal that nobody wants to be part of it. You can be the nicest of people on the planet but live your whole life without purpose, feeling empty inside. Then what's the point?

Life isn't promised, so you've got to celebrate. As media giant and philanthropist Oprah Winfrey said, "The more you praise and celebrate your life, the more there is in life to celebrate."

There's no point in taking a big bite out of life unless you take the time to savor the flavor. Some people never learn how to do enough of that. They let the belief that they aren't good enough hold them back from ever celebrating anything or from letting their true colors shine. No cake, no party!

So how did we get here?

Chapter 2

Let's Talk about Where it All Started

The best years of your life are the ones in which you decide your problems are your own. You do not blame them on your mother, the ecology, or the president. You realize that you control your own destiny.

—Dr. Albert Ellis

WE'RE born with a clean slate. Pure inside and out. The first six years of our lives are the formative years—the most critical stage—when we're molded into the kinds of human beings we'll become. In those first six years, we have very few options, and exercising our right to choose is very limited. We don't get to choose where we're born, who our parents are, or what religion we are born into. We don't even get to choose our names. We aren't free to just *be*. We get programmed into accepting and taking on anything and everything that's passed on to us by the two most important people in our lives at that stage, our moms and dads (or whoever our primary caregivers are). They dictate to us the societal and cultural standards of what's acceptable. And we conform with blind faith because from a very early age, all we want is their love and attention, and for that, we're willing to do anything without question.

So, we blend in to fit in, and somewhere along the way, we disappear. We somehow lose the path we were meant to take so we can grow fully into who we were meant to become. Our need to be loved outweighs our need to be anything else.

On average, a child hears ten times more negative messages than positive ones. As we grow older, in our teenage years, we start to feel a sense of identity developing, and we no longer want to blend in. We start to realize our parents aren't necessarily correct and that what they say isn't necessarily true. We start to think for ourselves. We rebel, or we become mute. Emotionally mute.

Love comes in many languages, and when we don't receive it in childhood, we spend the rest of our lives trying to make up for it. Many children are deprived of that love. Starved for it.

Those who are starving care less about death than they do about life, living their passions, expressing themselves, or being their true selves. The types of relationships we have with our family members carve out the way we feel about our self and our sense of self-worth. We need to be around them, and that need forms our personality, one that's born to please them. But there's another part of us, the one that tells you to just be you. A dual life emerges. The struggle between wanting those relationships and wanting an independent self is born.

Most kids live dual lives. They become disillusioned. They're afraid to be themselves for fear others will judge, blame, victimize, criticize, or reject them for who they are. We forget that the people who come into our path are simply mirrors for us to see who we have become—to learn something about ourselves.

And with the absence of feeling loved, anger emerges. We start to judge and compare and lose that sense of connectedness. We *want* to isolate and separate. And with that, "us versus them" or "me versus you" or "me versus the whole world" is created. When we're divided, we're weaker. The more division, the less love we feel, and our frustration is expressed through loveless acts—using words of hate or actions of harm on others. I see it over and over again in my private coaching practice—adults playing two different roles as a consequence of the inner struggle they've faced since childhood. Different parts of our personality and different voices in our head start their dialogues and arguments. The victim in us is born feeling guilty, and the judge in us is born to protect our ego.

As an adult, you get to the point where you become the one saying no to yourself all the time, ignoring your inner child. Telling her you have no time to attend to her needs, telling her to just suck it up. Soon enough, your emotional intelligence is on mute, and yet another separation is created between you and your inner child. Consider this: We think nothing of laughing in the face of a raging preschooler. Thus, we've inherited a tradition of discounting children's feelings simply because they are smaller, less rational, less experienced, and less powerful than the adults around them. The message they receive is that their feelings aren't important—that they don't count. The same reaction from an adult or a boss would not have us laughing at all.

I strongly believe adults have way more to learn from kids and teens than the other way around. As we grow, we unlearn some of the most amazing things, like curiosity, adventurousness, and carefree living. I learned from my younger siblings more than I can mention here. My sister inspires me and challenges me, and I love having her in my life. She reminds me of what it's like to be young and carefree again, something I sometimes forget as I "adult" more and more. My brother shows me what it's like to be truly passionate about something, and the way he defends his beliefs makes me question myself and how meek I am at times about standing up for what I want in my life. There's much in my life today I give my younger siblings credit for.

The childlike mind is a beautiful gift—a sponge that soaks up life. We need to reconnect with that child inside us, to remember to live in awe again, to remember it's a beautiful world out there!

The innocent girls and boys we were don't pretend they're having fun when they aren't. They don't pretend they like you when they don't. They're sincere, honest, and transparent in their emotions. They're fascinated with the world around them and awestruck by everything they see. They're unstoppable in the pursuit of their own versions of happiness and fun. All that disappears, though, when they're little girls and boys no longer. This brings tears to my eyes.

The innocent little girl or boy inside who's gone through childhood with all its good and bad events still has an enormous influence on how we live as adults. Our views of everything in our life and the world, of self-love, of our parents, and of our self-worth are all formulated through those childhood memories and experiences. Certain events get trapped in our subconscious minds and over time become what psychologists call emotional blocks. With every similar event we experience, that block hardens, the belief behind it being confirmed and reaffirmed. The next thing you know, our memory of the event itself is lost, but our reactions to life are based on how we processed it that very first time.

But there comes a point when enough is enough. It's time to wake up. Time to put the past in the past. Time to open our eyes and finally see. That is the journey of self-discovery or personal growth or awakening—call it what you like. It's a journey that involves a bit of pain as we fix all the mess we made while we learn to become fearless and start reconnecting again. Only when you make that conscious decision to wake up does your transformation truly begin. Transforming inside and discovering how to be alive comes from every little decision you make, every plan you execute and vice you quit. You re-create you!

The journey of self-discovery is a story of triumph over tribulation. It's a story of healing. Life constantly throws things at us to rock our boat, and our journey teaches us to find our even keel faster, so our boat doesn't topple over. How well you do with this whole journey depends on your well-being: emotionally, mentally, physically, and spiritually. It depends on your passionability.

Chapter 3

Which Type of Person Are You?

*For if you bake bread with indifference, you bake a
bitter bread that feeds but half man's hunger. And
if you grudge the crushing of the grapes, your grudge
distills a poison in the wine. And if you sing though
as angels, and love not the singing, you muffle man's
ears to the voices of the day and the voices of the night.*

—Khalil Gibran

IT's not about what happens to you; it's about how you react
to it. Imagine you have $86,400 in your bank account.
Now imagine someone steals $100 from you. Will you spend
more of the remaining money, the $86,300, to get your $100
back or catch or punish the guy who stole it? Or will you
say, "Forget it," and let it go? A participant in one of my
workshops jokingly said it depended on whether it was the
beginning or the end of the month!

So, now, let me ask you, which is more important: time
or money?

Time. Please tell me that was your answer. Time is the
only commodity you can't replace.

What if I say the $86,400 isn't money but instead is the number of seconds in a day? What if I say the thief is just a negative person who nags at you day in and day out, or it's the person in the elevator with the poker face who never says good morning back to you. Am I going to waste the rest of my day getting upset over him? It's the same thing when we give our attention to negative people and negativity in our life. So, it's a matter of choosing how much time you're going to spend on those negative people and those negative thoughts.

Giacomo Rizzolatti, an Italian neuroscientist, discovered that our minds have something called mirror neurons—motor cells that fire when someone else moves. The more active they are, the more empathetic you are. So around negative people, you'll detect that negativity, and it will impact you almost like secondhand smoking. So, stay away from negative people, and don't sweat the small stuff.

No matter what your level of education, age, experience, wealth, influence, who you know, or what car you drive, you'll be one of two kinds of people: the happy people or everybody else.

Happy people are part of the performance in a parade. They're the ones who make things happen.

Happy people change the world. Living in a state of inner peace and serenity is when you're happy for no particular reason. That's why you want to live from a place of happiness rather than live to attain happiness. Most people seek happiness from outside factors—from other people and things. When you're the generator rather than the consumer of happiness, you change your world and the world of people around you. It's all a state of mind, a state of true inner happiness.

In many shamanic societies, if you complained of being depressed, they would ask you one of four questions:

1. When did you stop dancing?

2. When did you stop singing?

3. When did you stop being enchanted by stories?

4. When did you stop finding comfort in the sweet territory of silence?

Happy people know to always honor their souls through dancing, singing, storytelling, and silence.

Happy people facing a challenge know you have to persevere. You don't keep your head down and be part of the problem. You hold your head up and continue to move forward. Happy people believe that when you throw your heart and soul into something without overanalyzing it, you can excel.

Happy people are also emotionally intelligent. I'm often asked what that really means. Here's my definition. It's the capacity from within to manage our own emotions and our inner potential for the sake of having better relationships and interactions with ourselves and with others.

When we feel an emotion, it stirs within us the urge to act. Our relationships and interactions with other people actually reshape our brain through something called neuroplasticity. It's like muscle memory. How we connect has a critical impact on us. For example, kids who are neglected during their early years tend to be less empathetic. When our brain is idle, its favorite soap opera to pass the time is to mull over our relationships. When someone with whom we are in a relationship doesn't emotionally nourish us on a regular basis, we can become chronically sad or angry with that person. The relationship becomes strained.

Happy people are conscious of their own impact on others and they take responsibility for their moods and how they are feeling. They know emotions are contagious, like the flu. We mirror others and feel with them. Mirror neurons reflect what we observe in others, allowing us to mimic them. This explains why we reflexively flinch when we see that someone else is about to get smacked or pinpricked. You've heard it yourself: when you're smiling, the whole world smiles back at you. We're all mirrors of one another. That's where empathy comes from.

Happy people are empathetic. They share and sense other people's emotions. They're tapped into their intuition and can feel hidden undertones others may not be revealing or may not even be aware they're feeling. This is one of the skills of a good life coach. Psychopaths have zero empathy. They find it difficult to recognize emotions like fear on other people's faces. Even as kids, they tend to be coldhearted.

To be empathetic means three things:

1. You notice others' emotional states.

2. You feel with them.

3. You're compelled into action to help them.

For this to happen, full attention needs to be present so a real connection can take place. Distraction makes you miss clues. The eyes are the windows to the soul, as they say, and it's through the eyes and body language that emotions are revealed.

Happy people are those who focus on outcomes. They focus on how much they want to do what they are doing. They focus on benefits. They see obstacles as mere challenges they have to overcome. For them, it is a matter of when, not if.

Happy people are passionate about something. For a passionate person who wants to grow, the whole world becomes a garden, and everything in it a chance to become curious about what would happen if he planted it. If she wants to learn, the whole world becomes a school, and everything in it an opportunity for her to further her education. If he wants to paint, the whole world becomes a canvas, and everybody in it a muse to inspire him. Happy people change the world.

To a happy person, happiness and the excuse to smile are found everywhere and in everything. If all else fails, they will just clench a pencil in their teeth, which will force their faces to smile and automatically make them feel happy. Go on; grab a pencil and try it yourself. I know you want to! When you smile at life, half the smile is for your face, and the other half is for life, and karma is a beautiful thing.

Daniel Goleman, a psychologist and a leader in the field of emotional intelligence, describes how US Army Lt. Col. Christopher Hughes made his soldiers kneel on one knee, point their rifles toward the ground, and ... smile! He did it when they were surrounded by hundreds of Iraqis who were pressing in toward the platoon, shouting and angry, fearing that the soldiers were there to arrest their leader. Hughes ordered his soldiers to slowly walk backward and away, still smiling. The crowd's mood morphed[1]. That's the power of a smile. It makes a hostile environment safer, breaching barriers of language and culture. And that was also a sign of emotional intelligence on the part of the commanding officer.

Going a step further, when you laugh, you set off multiple positive events in your body. Stress hormone levels decrease; muscles relax; your immunity system gets a boost; immunoglobulin A antibodies increase; natural killer cells, or NK, which destroy tumor cells increase; and those are just a few of the benefits. Laughing is also soul medicine. In laughter-yoga classes, it's hilarious how you'll start with a fake laugh and end up in stitches from laughing for real within minutes. Find one in your neighborhood and give it a try.

Last night, I fell asleep as I watched a firefly hover over the mosquito net covering my bed at the resort I was staying at in Talalla, Sri Lanka. I'd never seen one before. How magical! I woke up early to get ready for my yoga class, and it was raining. The bathrooms in the resort where I was staying are open concept, with no roofs. I literally showered in the rain. How sensational! As I got dressed, I saw a family of monkeys jumping from tree to tree. How invigorating! Here I am writing my book on passion and happiness, and everything around me is showing me what a wonderful world I live in. Happy people notice the small things and take pleasure in the noticing.

The second category is everybody else. They are those who stand on the sidewalk and watch as life goes by. Starting really early, we get hit with this thing called life and get knocked down to our knees. Then it hits us again and again. We start to become afraid. We learn to be fearful so we can protect ourselves. Fear seeps into our minds and poisons our lives. Growing up, we get bruised and battered; we're messed up by the time we're adults and start to have a lot of baggage. We start to consciously or unconsciously disrupt the peace ourselves. We want to rebel, cause chaos, and hurt other people, other animals, even ourselves. Drug our senses so we don't feel anything anymore. We just want to be entertained externally so we're distracted from what's happening internally. We become disconnected from ourselves and the world around us.

Sometimes we fear the things we desire the most because we're terrified we'll mess them up. But think of what you'd be missing out on if you didn't even try. Some of the scariest moments in life have nothing to do with things like jumping off a cliff or walking barefoot on burning coals. They are about facing your demons or having the moral courage to walk away from something you know isn't right.

If you've seen the movie *Catwoman*, consider the difference between Patience Phillips and Catwoman—the two roles played by Halle Berry. Patience is full of self-doubt. She's a talented artist, but instead of unleashing her full potential, she is settling for a job where her boss bullies her. She's gorgeous—it's Halle Berry, after all—yet she's insecure, with minimal self-esteem and no positive body image of herself. Her self-worth is totally dependent on what others think of her and her work. Catwoman, on the other hand, is out-of-this-world confident in that tight black leather outfit. She's full of self-confidence, knowing she can do whatever she wants; she's capable and self-sufficient, and her self-worth isn't dependent on others' opinions of her. It's all a matter of self-doubt versus self-belief.

Here's a quick rundown of how the two types of people compare with each other:

- Happy people are proactive. Everybody else is the reactive type.

- Proactive people are ones who say, "I can," and "I will." Reactive people say, "I can't."

- The typical question a proactive person will ask about anything is, "Why not?" A reactive person will ask, "Why me?"

- Proactive people listen. Reactive people just talk, talk, talk. And they ignore you in the process. They talk to you only to give their side of the story. In a conversation, they're waiting for you to stop talking so it'll be their turn to talk. That's assuming they didn't interrupt you repeatedly to get started with their stories in the first place.

- Proactive people are results-focused, results-oriented. Reactive people focus on blaming, complaining, and making excuses.

Do you know reactive people? Maybe at work? Do you run away from work and get home and there's one there, too? They're everywhere.

The average person complains a lot. If you think that's not you, try this: wear a wristband on one hand, and every time you catch yourself complaining, move it to the other hand. See for yourself how much of a big whiner you are. Challenge yourself to go two weeks without moving it.

We prefer to complain and suffer from our self-chosen addiction to anxiety and panic attacks than to apply ourselves to a routine of small and simple daily commitments that could be the ticket to our salvation and growth.

Here's a fun thing you can do to help eradicate this epidemic: Have a complaints jar at home or in your office. Every single time someone complains about anything, they have to put money in the jar. When the jar is filled to the top, the last person who puts in money needs to treat you, the whole family at home, or the team in the office to dinner. This is meant to make people visually realize how negative they're being.

Proactive people are authoritative, not authoritarian. When you're authoritative, you set limits, but you're flexible; you explain why or why not. Reactive people—authoritarians—offer no explanations. They expect obedience. They have zero flexibility. They remind me of my dad and his favorite reply to me when I was a kid: "No means no, end of discussion, because I said so." When it was time for me to go to university, he said, "You have two options, Randa: Beirut or Beirut. Pick!" That's being authoritarian. I love him still.

Lastly, proactive people come from a place of love for everything they do, whereas reactive people come from a place of fear. We can make fear-based decisions, or we can make love-based ones. Decisions can be powered by passion. Now, as adults, nobody's going to call us out for being afraid because we've learned to camouflage our fear with excuses, very legitimate excuses like "I don't have time," "I'm so stressed," or "I don't have the money to follow my dream." But deep down inside, you don't pursue your dreams or have a life that's powered by passion because you're afraid, and it is much easier to stay in your comfort zone. If you went all out and told the world what you wanted to do, you might fail, and everyone would know. We are afraid of rejection; we're afraid of not being good enough. I could wait to publish this book until it's absolutely perfect, but you wouldn't ever get to read it because it's never going to be perfect. Look at the iPhone. If Apple cofounder Steve Jobs had waited until his idea was perfect, would we have iPhones today?

Which type of person do you think or believe you are? And which one would other people around you say you are?

The fact of the matter is, we spend our whole lives fighting and struggling to have people accept us for who we are as we are, yet we spend the same amount of energy and time hiding who we are as we are!

Without discipline, we can't solve anything, we can't reach our goals, and we definitely can't live our dreams. Discipline is the difference between proactive and reactive people. And suffering is part of a disciplined life. It's one of the four noble truths that Buddha taught. He said, "Life is suffering." Once we accept that as a fact, we start to act more proactively; we face our problems and challenges head-on, along with all the pain that comes with them. Most of us are unwilling to tolerate the pain or discomfort that comes with the long journey of pursuing a dream or a goal. We can't wait long enough to solve issues in a conscious, proactive manner, so we react unconsciously, without discipline. We become reactive. And blind people don't see any goals or dreams anymore.

Chapter 4

Powered by Passion,
What Would You Do?

Without passion, man is a mere latent force and possibility, like the flint which awaits the shock of the iron before it can give forth its spark.

—Henri Frédéric Amiel

GET comfortable in your seat. Take a deep breath, and as you release that breath, let yourself relax. Notice where you might be tense, breathe into that place, and let the tension go with the exhale of your next breath. Take another deep breath, and as you exhale, start to imagine.

Imagine you live to be one hundred years old. Imagine you're at your milestone birthday party. Imagine the place. Imagine what you look like. Now imagine yourself moments before you're about to blow out the candles. Who are the people standing all around you singing for you at your party? Is it a surprise party? Where is it? Imagine what thoughts are going through your head at that moment. What accomplishments have you done in your life? What are you most proud of? What kind of a person are you? What are you most ashamed of? Do you have any regrets? Who is the first person at your party to give a toast, and what are they saying about you? Who else wants to speak?

Now imagine you're asked to give a speech about your happy and successful life. What would you like to share with everyone? You think and reflect for a moment before you start speaking. You're looking back at your life with such great joy, pride, and confidence. You reflect on the different chapters of your life. What have you accomplished? What are you leaving behind? What will you be remembered by? What imprint, no matter how large or small, did you have on the people in your life: your children, your loved ones, your community, and the world you live in?

Now take a deep breath, breathing in this experience, remembering what you need to remember and come back to the room you're in right now. I invite you to journal about this before you continue reading.

This is who you are now, years and decades before that birthday party. Take a moment to think about where you are in life now. What do you do on a daily basis? What's the most exciting thing about your life now? What takes up the biggest chunk of your free time? Do you realize that what you do today will impact who you are at one hundred?

Find a mirror and look straight into your own eyes for a few moments. Now ask yourself, "If I can change one thing in my life today so I can achieve that life I just visualized, what would it be?"

Okay, if I know anything about exercises in a self-help book, I know this: nobody does them! But I also know that if you make an honest effort and do every single one in this book, you'll be massively rewarded.

This is an exercise about clarity. When you have a clear vision of what you want to make of your life, choice becomes easy. When you know what you're passionate about and what makes your heart sing, you're pulled into action powered by passion, by that vision you have for your life. Always choose in favor of your passion, no matter what. When you have a meaningful why, the how takes care of itself.

Once upon a Dream in Ancaster

Every great dream begins with a dreamer. Always remember, you have within you the strength, the patience, and the passion to reach for the stars to change the world.

—Unknown

One dark, quiet night in Ancaster, Ontario, I had a dream. And through that dream, I found my calling.

While I was still living in Canada and still in my short-lived marriage, I went to an intensive women's retreat. It was the best thing I've ever done for myself, without a doubt. Every woman deserves to experience something like that. That's why I run my own retreats and experiential learning events now.

On the last night there, I had a powerful and vivid dream. I dreamed I was helping a blind handywoman. She couldn't complete the task of hanging some pictures on a wall that I'd requested of her, and her company policy was to call in another handywoman who could finish the job. I wasn't going to let her do that. I told her that I would help instead. I took her by the hand and showed her how to do the task. Somewhere in the middle, I looked at my husband and wondered what he was doing in my life exactly and why he was even there. That was the whole dream.

I jolted out of my sleep with a mixture of excitement, shock, and disbelief. My heart was practically beating out of my chest. In the pitch darkness around me, my eyes were wide-open. I saw clearly as I was repeating these words to myself: "Oh my, God is speaking to me through this dream, telling me what to do. This is my calling, my life's mission. I can see it."

When I was back in class, I shared my dream and asked the facilitator why she didn't give retreats like this to young adults or teens, and she said it wasn't her calling. In my head, I said, *Well, now it's mine!*

Over time, this dream had a profound impact and meaning for me as the idea of what I was supposed to do with this message became more and more concrete. I wanted to help women see a better way of life by finding their passions and empowering their lives. I wanted to help young people live their lives with passion and purpose. I wanted them to tap into their highest potential and know there was nothing they couldn't do. I wanted to awaken the humanity in people and have them live meaningful lives. But I needed to empower myself first. I needed to get out of the marriage I was in, too. And I did. A few years later, I decided to move back to Abu Dhabi after having another dream with a vivid message that I needed to leave Canada and go back to the UAE. I wanted to bring all the good things I'd experienced and learned on my own self-empowerment journey back to my part of the world, to you.

Let me tell you, since that dream, I haven't had any trouble making choices regarding what I want to do with my life. This is it. It's crystal clear to me. And this is life: It doesn't give you what you need. It gives you what you focus on. So, what is it you focus on in your life? Is it your outcomes and results, as achievers do—the 20 percent of people —or is it the obstacles, excuses, and fears the non-achievers —the other 80 percent—do?

Asking yourself what it is you're most passionate about in life is probably the most important question you could ever ask. I went through years of not knowing what it was I truly loved and enjoyed doing. I believed if I was really passionate about something, I couldn't live without it. It meant I couldn't allow anyone to take it away from me or try to stop me from doing it.

For the longest time, I had no passion. Yes, I loved a ton of things. I had a career as an interior designer for almost a decade; I became a design consultant in Toronto, and then I got into real estate. But I now know that I wasn't really as passionate about any of these things as I am about what I saw to be my life's mission through that dream and what I'm doing now. You're passionate about something when you know you have to do it every day for the rest of your life.

Your passion is what ignites your fire for life. It's what gets you out of bed every morning, saying, "Yes, another day of doing what I love." It's like the North Star, always guiding you in the right direction, showing you where your true north is, the direction you have chosen for your life. The direction that comes naturally to you and that you effortlessly work toward. It occupies your mind even when you're sleeping.

Unlike obsessions that may have negative implications, your passions inspire and drive you forward, making you want to become only better. They make you feel warm and fuzzy inside. They bring that buzz to every cell in your body. They're all you want to think about. They're all you want to do.

Passion is energy, and without energy, nothing happens. How many people do you know who are living but aren't alive? I'd rather live one day of intense passion for life, for what I'm doing and for who I am, than a whole eternity in mediocrity.

By now you may be thinking, *I'm a full-time employee with little time for much else,* or *I'm a student and barely have time for school, homework, exams, and chores,* or *I'm a mother who has to juggle taking care of my kids, a husband, and a home.* I was in your shoes and didn't have the time for that kind of thing, either. I was too busy sulking, complaining, feeling sorry for myself, and blaming others for my misery. I thought this whole passion business was all fine and dandy, but there was nothing I could think of that I was doing that fit the description of a passionate life. Moreover, I had all these other things in my life that I needed to take care of, like keeping a marriage together, making money, and managing the weight gain that was getting out of control.

I looked at other people I knew who were passionate about something and felt envious. I felt like a loser because I was living an empty life with no passion. My life had no meaning. Those thoughts kept going through my head nonstop until that night at the women's retreat when I had that dream—the dream that changed everything.

So, what would you love to be doing in life? Who do you want to be? Wouldn't you want to know what really makes your heart sing? What would make your life a ten out of ten?

It may be pretty daunting to think you have to know it all now. You may be thinking, *I'm only twenty or thirty years old. How the hell am I supposed to know what I'm going to do with the rest of my life? I can barely decide what I'm going to wear this weekend or cook for dinner! How should I know now what impact my life will make by the time I'm one hundred?*

I hear you. I understand. Let's step back for a second and ask why it's so important to know our passion and what we desire most in life.

When you do that thing you love, and when you love what you do, you become a happy person. Happy people change the world, and we need a lot more happy people around us. That's why!

A body of research on happiness shows that only 10 percent of our happiness can be attributed to outside factors like health, money, relationships, and whatever else you want to blame for your unhappiness[2]. And let's face it, when you're in a negative mood, you're ready to blame it on anything, be it the traffic, the neighbors, a coworker, the rain, the planets' alignment, or your mother.

Finding what you're truly passionate about doing is the most important thing in life. Oprah Winfrey says that if you don't know what it is, finding it should be your full-time job. No excuses.

Passion is what brought us the stunning art of Salvador Dali and Michelangelo, the dazzling plays of Shakespeare, the greatest movies of Hollywood, the innovation of Steve Jobs, the mesmerizing music of Chopin and the Beatles, the brilliant inventions of Thomas Edison, and the genius discoveries of Albert Einstein. Without passion, none of that would exist. It's passion that stirs the very soul of a person to get them out of bed and to pour hours, days, years, and even decades of their life into something.

For example, the making of *The Birth of a Nation*, a movie about the life story of Nat Turner, took only twenty-seven days to shoot. But a solid ten years of work preceded that. Everyone who worked on it had never worked so hard before and had never wanted to. But they did it because they were bound by their passion for the story. That's what being powered by passion is all about. Knowledge and expertise alone aren't enough to make a Steve Jobs or an Oprah Winfrey. Passion is the secret sauce.

If you want more out of life, you need to become more. Your why has to be worth it. Your passion has to give you meaning that will overcome any how.

To become what we are capable of becoming is the only end in life.

—Robert Louis Stevenson

In his brilliant book *The Outliers*, Malcolm Gladwell explains that to become a master at anything, you have to spend a total of ten thousand hours doing it[3]. That translates to ten years, give or take. That's what the Beatles did in Hamburg, Germany, playing gigs night after night as a no-name band. By the time their stroke of luck hit, they were all geared up with their ten thousand hours. That's what Bill Gates did. He spent all his teenage years working all night long at a nearby university computer room. By the time he was twenty and his lucky strike came, he had ten thousand hours of coding under his belt.

So if I am to become a master at anything and therefore have to spend ten years of my life working at it, wouldn't it be marvelous if that thing I'm doing is a passion? That I'm actually in love with it? I can't imagine for a second that Bill Gates was forced to go code in the middle of the night. He gravitated to it. His parents wondered why he always had a hard time waking up to go to school. The Beatles weren't forced to perform every night. They wanted to.

Maybe there is no difference between a passion and an obsession. There can't be a work/life balance once you're engrossed in your passion. Anger and frustration become your fuel and motivation. A challenge or a fight gives you more juice to continue working; figuring out how to live that passion is more powerful than any motivational speech. When someone tells you no, it boosts a whole other level of tenacity and perseverance in you to keep you going. I'd say we all need a Simon Cowell in our lives. I sob when watching those talent videos more than I do over the corniest chick flicks. Nothing can stop you when you know you have it in you and you know what it is you want out of life—that passion that brings life to life itself!

A few years ago, I was in Fiji to attend a Tony Robbins "Life and Wealth Mastery" event. They took us to Sunday Mass. Of all the topics in the whole wide world, the priestess chose to speak about being you. "Just be who you are!" she said. "Be yourself!" I mean, can you believe it? It was short and to the point. At this point, I had just started Be You International, my life coaching practice. I thought, *What are the chances of me traveling halfway across the world to attend Mass and to have it be about being you. Hey, universe, I hear the message loud and clear!* And to be you is to live a life where you're powered by your passion.

Deciding on Your "What"
and Setting Intentions

When you engage in work that taps your talent and fuels your passion—that rises out of a great need in the world that you feel drawn by conscience to meet —therein lies your voice, your calling, your soul's code.

—Stephen R. Covey

A primary ingredient to your happiness formula is finding out the answer to "What is your vision?" What do you want to do with your life? What is it you're meant to do in the world, to make your legacy? What's your purpose? Mark Twain said, "The two most important days in your life are the day you are born and the day you find out why." Knowing exactly what it is you'll create is key to your being happy.

October 1, 1971 was the grand opening of Walt Disney World in Orlando, Florida. A close family friend told Walt Disney's wife, Lillian, that he wished Walt would have been there with them to see the opening. She replied, "He did see it; that's why it's here."

We all have a calling. We all have a passion. And there are so many signs to help us find out what it is. But many times, we choose not to listen. Only the very few will do what it takes to slow down enough to listen to the signs and to understand the direction they're pointing toward. Once you know what your life's work is, your whole world will come alive, be more vibrant than ever before. You'll wake up with more energy and enthusiasm. All of a sudden, you'll have no time to waste and nothing else to think about. You have to have clarity. You'll never be able to hit a target you can't see or meet a goal you can't visualize.

I heard Tony Robbins in one of his live events say, "Ask stupid questions, and you'll get stupid answers." Here are ten smart questions to help you get started:

1. If you could make a thirty-second speech to the entire world, what would you say?

2. If you had all the money and time in the world, what kind of work would you still do?

3. When you turn seventy-five, what will matter most to you?

4. What do you regret most so far, and how can you apply the lesson you learned from that regret to your life today?

5. If you lost everything tomorrow, whose arms would you want to run into? Does that person know how much they mean to you?

6. When will you be good enough for you? Is there a time when you'll accept everything about yourself?

7. What will people say about you at your funeral, and is that different from what you'd like them to say and remember you by?

8. If you were at heaven's gate and God asked you, "Why should I let you in?" What would you say?

9. What small thing would you love to do often to make someone's day better?

10. What do you believe stands between you and complete happiness? And if that obstacle magically disappeared, what would you do?

We start the process of finding our passion by getting clear about what we want. It's a process of closing the gap between where you are now and where you want to be. The above questions will keep you thinking for days. The answer may immediately come to you, for the heart knows what it loves. Your soul knows how it wants to be of service. But if you're still not sure, the following steps should help you.

What results are you committed to creating in your life? What dreams and kind of lifestyle do you want to be yours? What's the ultimate target?

Write down a minimum of three dreams or things you desire to have or be or do in each of the following areas. (Of course, you can add more areas as you see fit.)

1. Family

2. Career/life mission

3. Fun activities

4. Relationships

5. Making a difference

6. Wellness in four areas: heart, mind, body, and soul.

Write in the present tense, as if you are already living them. Now, what are the beliefs that will empower you to create these results? Write those down, too.

Writing your goals, plans, and dreams down is important. It's not enough to have them in your head. In 1953, Yale University took a poll of its graduating class. They found that only 3 percent of the students wnts had done proper goal setting—finding out what they wanted—and had written their goals down before graduation. Twenty years later, those same 3 percent had earned 50 percent of the total income of their class combined.

Finding Your Big Juicy "Why"

He who has a why to live for can bear almost any how.

—Friedrich Nietzsche

Once you know what it is you want to do, it's just as important to figure out why. Without knowing why you're doing anything you do, it will be difficult to pull through the tough times, and, oh yes, those will keep coming at you. Your conscience is what drives your why. Just because you're happy doesn't mean the whole world will turn pink and rosy for you. But knowing why I do the work I do has pulled me through many challenges and rough times. The last few years have been like a learning curve that was less of a curve and more like a straight line going up! Every little step that had to be taken to set up my business, Be You International, in a place that's still relatively new to the world of life coaching and experiential learning has been a huge ordeal. Many things I simply had no clue how to do, but I knew how to figure it out, I knew who to ask, and I knew why. That why is the most important thing to know. Without it, many times I would have packed my bags and called it quits. My why made me persevere and kept me moving forward.

Where are you now? What kind of results are you producing now compared to the past? Why change anything at all? What's holding you back? Are you fearful of the future? What beliefs do you currently hold that make you feel stuck where you are? Are you committed this time to making these results happen, unlike other times in the past? Why?

Bill Levacy, a performance consultant, came up with "the secret formula" to getting exactly what you want in your life. It's also an integral part of the Passion Test, which is my absolute favorite tool in my coaching practice. The formula has three steps.

1. Intention: Know what your intentions are. All the work covered in this chapter so far helps you to develop clarity. That's the most critical step. Be clear about what you want. You must always be very clear and specific about what you want. The Prophet Mohammad said, "Actions are by intentions, and for every person is what he intended."

2. Attention: Intention without action means nothing. I meet many people with great ideas that go nowhere. They have the ideas but lack the power of execution. What's the point? What you put your attention on grows stronger. Attention is focus, which drives you into action.

3. No tension: Let go and relax. There's no point in stressing over how things will manifest in your life. You need to take it all with open arms because the universe may have something even better in store for you, and everything comes to you in good time.

Clarifying the "How"

*As I walked out the door toward the gate that would
lead to my freedom, I knew if I didn't leave my bitterness and hatred behind, I'd still be in prison.*

—Nelson Mandela

Once you know what you want and why you want it, you'll
have clarity about your direction in life. That clarity is critical. How can you ever hit a target you can't see?

What's left now is to ask how. How are you going to
achieve what you want? Your time for reflection and thinking was covered in the first two questions; now it's time for
action. How is determined by your discipline. This is the
time for a plan. Not just any kind of plan, but an action
plan. And not any kind of action plan, but a massive one, a
plan that will propel you forward. There are so many com-
ponents to a plan and so many ways to implement it. But
what's most important is to write it down.

This is the time to close the gap and hit the road running.
Now that you're clear about what you want, the next step is
to turn those big beautiful dreams into goals and measurable
objectives. *Measurable* means getting into the nitty-gritty.
What exactly do you want? How much of it do you want?
And how soon do you want it?

Janet Bray Attwood, in her book *The Passion Test: The
Effortless Path to Discovering Your Life Purpose*, says clarity
shows up in your life, but only to the extent that you are

clear. And clarity requires making choices. That's how the law of attraction works. You need to be specific. It's sort of like ordering at a restaurant. Do you ever walk in, take a seat, look at the menu for a while, and then tell the waiter, "Get me something delicious"? Who does that? Or do you hop on a plane without knowing the destination, never mind packing a bag for a trip without knowing what kind of weather and trip you're packing for? It's the same with the universe. It will give you what you want.

Before you start to feel overwhelmed by everything you're writing down and like, you have to abandon your current life. Remember that what you're dealing with is 80 percent psychology and 20 percent mechanics. With the right state of mind, you can achieve anything. There are no unresourceful people, only unresourceful states of mind, so make sure you surround yourself with people who will support you and your dreams. Happiness comes from progress. Progress shows up in the form of growth and a sense of contribution. You can be held back from succeeding by your own mind-set and lack of following through, day in and day out. Nothing can trump perseverance and tenacity.

Successful people do what lazy people don't. Even if they hate having to do a particular task, their habits and commitment are stronger than their dislike or discomfort. Their discipline is powered by their vision and purpose. Their drive comes from within. They're powered by passion. Seth Godin, a thought leader in the world of marketing, is known for getting up early every day, having his cup of coffee, and then sitting at his desk to write for sixteen hours so that he posts a blog every day. Every single day.

Without commitment, nothing happens. As soon as you commit to a big dream and really go after it, your subconscious creative mind will come up with great ideas on how to make it happen. You'll start attracting the people, resources, and opportunities you need in your life to make your dream come true. Big dreams not only inspire you, but they also compel others to want to play big, too. Being aware of our freedom to choose for ourselves and the power to do what we choose excites us with possibilities, but it also terrifies us because of the responsibilities involved. So again, make sure you're surrounded with people who like to play in the same awesomeness circles you want to be a part of.

As you practice those habits, be easy on yourself, and trust that you're removing the blocks to reaching your goals. To keep your subconscious focused on what you want, close your eyes, think about each goal, and ask yourself, "What is one thing I could do today to move toward the achievement of this goal?" Write down your answers and take those actions.

A very powerful way to do this is through vision boards. I've created many vision boards over the years. One of my favorites, which I have as my phone wallpaper image, has the words "The beauty of being you" on it. I made it just before I started Be You International, my life coaching business in the UAE. The little magic that starts to happen once you are crystal clear on your goals and dreams is nothing short of, well, miraculous. You have to be able to see your goal so you can hit the bull's-eye. Vision boards really make that happen.

Your what is powered by your vision; your why is powered by your conscience; and your how is powered by discipline. The common denominator is passion. And now you are powered by passion!

Think about that and give it a shot. It can take you a couple of hours to a couple of days to get it all sorted out. Then you're all set, and it's time to let your true potential manifest in your life.

That's what living powered by passion looks like. You know what you want; you know exactly why you want it; and you have a kick-ass plan to get there. Own that plan and cheer yourself on at the milestones.

Don't be like most people, who are addicted to anxiety and worry. They'd rather have the pain of a life that's boring them to death than the dread of taking small and simple daily steps in the right direction along the path to living their passion. Most people fail to achieve their goals in life for one simple reason: they never take the first steps. Many books are left unwritten, many instruments are left unplayed, and many dreams are left collecting dust on back shelves.

Don't be that person. Keep yourself in what Tony Robbins calls "a peak state." From that state, only the best results can be achieved. Resolve and commit. Keep reminding yourself of the decision you made, and stick with it. Take immediate and consistent action.

Do everything you do with passion. Let it be what powers you from the minute you get up in the morning, throughout your day, and till the moment you fall asleep at night. Shower with passion. Brush your teeth with passion. Exercise with passion. Speak with passion.

Passion and love both come from the heart. By living a life aligned with your passions, you will love the life you live because you're always doing what you love!

Emotion comes from the Latin word *emovere*, meaning *to disturb*. We think, then feel, and then act—in that order. Don't let emotions disturb your mojo. Be in charge. Show your mind who's boss, and decide to live happily ever after.

Part II

Cocoons

Our deepest fear is not that we are inadequate. Our deepest fear is that we are powerful beyond measure. It is our light, not our darkness that most frightens us. We ask ourselves, 'Who am I to be brilliant, gorgeous, talented, fabulous?' Actually, who are you not to be? You are a child of God. Your playing small does not serve the world. There is nothing enlightened about shrinking so that other people won't feel insecure around you. We are all meant to shine, as children do. We were born to make manifest the glory of God that is within us. It's not just in some of us; it's in everyone. And as we let our own light shine, we unconsciously give other people permission to do the same. As we are liberated from our own fear, our presence automatically liberates others.

—Marianne Williamson, A Return to Love

Chapter 5

That F*cking *F* Word

It's a heart afraid of breaking
that never learns to dance...

It's the dream afraid of waking
that never takes the chance...

And the soul afraid of dying
that never learns to live.

—Bette Midler, "The Rose"

have brought up fear a few times already, so let's talk some more about the elephant in the room.

Fear can destroy our psychology and immobilize us from taking action. All of us experience fear in some context during our lives: fear of rejection, fear of success or failure, fear of love or losing love, fear of being alone, or fear of the unknown. Fear is hardwired into our DNA, and nothing will take it away. The secret is learning how to use it instead of letting fear hold us back or destroy our life.

When my younger sister was about three years old, she'd jump off the edge of the swimming pool, arms and legs flapping, without a worry in the world. The following summer, though, she stood in the same place, unable to make the jump. Something had shifted in that one-year gap. Something made her think jumping wasn't okay the way it used to be. What happened?

As we grow, the concept of fear grows with us. It's triggered by innocent comments from adults like "Watch out" or "Be careful." Kids don't understand how to attach these comments to specific situations; instead, generalizing them so that they apply to everything. Fortunately, I was there to give my sister encouragement, to hold her hand, and jump with her. Within minutes, she was okay again. Sometimes we had to go through the same thing again the following day to get her to jump in.

That can happen to us at any age. If you dig deep enough, you'll realize that fear stops you from doing many things. We don't want to call it fear, though, so we mask it with all sorts of other things. We come up with all sorts of stories to hide it.

Fear stopped me from doing a lot of things. The mask I hid behind was that I was a shy person. My friend once told me that was the biggest lie I told myself. I didn't understand her then. Now, the more I think about what she said and how that mask really did stop me from doing so many fun things, I'm able to admit how true her observation was.

Here are some examples of people you've heard of who didn't let their bullshit stories stop them from achieving their dreams.

Did you know that actor Tom Cruise is dyslexic? He was diagnosed when he was only seven years old. Dyslexia is a learning disability, and it made him unable to perform well in school. With his auditions as an actor, he had to put in extra effort to read and memorize scripts. Now he's one of the most successful Hollywood stars and produces his own movies. Do you think he would have gotten anywhere if he had feared his disability or if he had worried about what others would think of him?

Sir Richard Branson is dyslexic, too. That impairment didn't stop him from becoming one of the most famous English businessmen. He is best known for his Virgin Group, which comprises more than four hundred companies.

Rowan Atkinson is the actor famous for his character Mr. Bean. As a kid, he had speech problems. He stuttered and had difficulty saying the letter *B*. He compensated by over-articulating it. He even used it in his comedy performances.

Anti-apartheid revolutionary Nelson Mandela was still a teen when he attended a tribal ceremony. A tribal elder stood up and said, "These are our young men. They are our future, but the truth is they are second-class citizens. They will always be boys." When Mandela heard that, he made the decision to change South Africa. That one decision changed the world forever. If he had feared the elders and what they thought of young boys, would he have made that kind of resolve at such a young age?

In the publishing world, twelve publishing houses rejected John Grisham's first book, *A Time to Kill*. Jack Canfield and Mark Victor Hansen's *Chicken Soup for the Soul: 101 Stories to Open the Heart and Rekindle the Spirit* was rejected one hundred and forty times.

In the science world, Charles Darwin was told he would amount to nothing and be a disgrace. Thomas Edison was told he was too stupid to learn. Albert Einstein did not speak until late in his childhood, at the age of four, and all his teachers told him he would never amount to much. He used to say he was aware that he was not particularly intelligent, but he knew he was very curious, and it was that curiosity that enabled him to do all the great work that he accomplished.

In the entertainment world, Walt Disney was fired and told he lacked imagination and had no original ideas. Oprah Winfrey was told she had no TV presence. She lived her childhood in poverty and was sexually abused, but she never lost sight of her passion and the vision she had for her life.

Larry Page and Sergey Brin, the cofounders of Google, started off in their garage and took on the seemingly impossible task of competing against internet giant Yahoo!. Look at them now. The list goes on and on.

We all love stories. We make them up all the time. Some are happy stories, and some … Well, some are just bullshit stories. And you have one. Yes, you do; don't argue with me. What's the bullshit story you keep telling yourself that stands in the way of achieving your dreams and living the life you truly want?

> *Being powerful is like being a lady. If you have to tell people you are, you aren't.*
>
> —Margaret Thatcher

Everyone has a story. The words of that story have their own power. They work so that you believe your story even when circumstances change. You believe your story and defend it until it becomes an integral part of your life, to the point at which you start to believe the story is you and you are the story. Ego and story intertwine, and the next thing you know, there's a bullshit festival going on!

The dream that once upon a time was vibrant and wanted to happen becomes a distant thought. Your story tells you the dream is ridiculous. It tells you that you can't do it. Your ego plants doubt in your mind about whether you even deserve it. Who do you think you are? It's beyond you. It's not safe. Stick to what you know. Dreaming big is for others.

Many awesome lives are lived in vain. Many beautiful dreams are surrendered to oblivion—all because we don't believe in ourselves—even when others told us to go for it. It breaks my heart to see that happening so often to so many.

> *The fear of death is fear of time, and the fear of time is, deeply, the fear of unlived moments, an unlived life.*
>
> —Osho

So, what is your bullshit story, and who would you be without that bullshit story? What would you achieve? What will it take for you to leap across the gap between where you are now and where you want to be? Have faith. Step up!

For things to change for you, you must change. It's not what happens to you; it's what you do that makes all the difference. If you want to change a behavior, an emotional pattern, or a feeling in the moment, you can.

But first, you have to have the conviction that you can change. That's a choice you're making for yourself. Once you've made that choice, you need to interrupt the pattern of the negative habit or emotional response that you want to change. Get out of your own head. Move out of the way of change. Let it happen. Do something else. Only then, can you create a new, more empowering alternative to the negative habit or feeling.

Picture a kid who wants to paint the walls with crayons. You can't tell her to stop without giving her a convincing just-as-juicy alternative, like a huge sketchbook. Simple.

When you fall back—and everyone does—pick yourself up, rinse, and repeat. When stuck, don't ask those old foolish questions: "Why me?" or "If I'm failing, isn't that an example of not being able to do it?" Instead, ask a more helpful question: "What's next for me?"

Just by switching words a little, you can open so much that was closed before. Replace "No way" with "Maybe," and see what happens. Try it, just for fun!

It takes a lot of energy to rock a chair or swing a swing, but you still remain in the same spot. It's the same with worrying. You spend a ton of time consumed by it, and it gets you nowhere. The Italian word for worry is *preoccupare*, and I like it because it gives me a visual of a mind *occupied* with things that are in the way of my happiness.

Frowning triggers the secretion of stress-inducing hormones like cortisol, adrenaline, and chemicals that weaken your immune system, making you susceptible to depression, anxiety, and high blood pressure. Smiling, on the other hand, decreases these substances and increases stress-reducing chemicals in your body such as endorphins and dopamine, which boost your immunity, relax your muscles, reduce aches and pains, and accelerate healing.

So now it's time for a new beginning. Now it's time to put an expiration date on the worrying and the blaming. No more pointing fingers at parents, society, religion, government, friends, spouses, or kids. Now it's time to remember that you can choose who you want to be, what you want to do, and how you'll live your life. You might fail; that's a given because life will keep kicking you in the gut just to test your commitment, but try again tomorrow and again the day after that. Don't hope; have faith in yourself and your abilities. Faith is fearless and has a more powerful vibe to it than hope. It already believes that you are capable of anything you set your mind to, as opposed to hope, which may or may not necessarily believe that what you are hoping for is possible. Take the energy you'd be spending to complain, pout, and bitch and moan about whatever it is, and put it into creativity and making something beautiful in your life.

Sigmund Freud said the purpose of life is to find pleasure. Alfred Adler said it's to find power. But I truly believe the purpose of life is to find meaning. Meaning in everything you do. Meaning at work—knowing you're making a difference in the world, and meaning in love—knowing you're making a difference in someone else's life. The purpose of life is to have a purpose!

Toddlers say no, and they mean it. They keep repeating it over and over like it's their way to assert their independence. It's how they discover the joy and power of establishing their little identities. As we go through life, we have to keep practicing saying no. The older we get, the harder it gets. We're conditioned to please. In some schools, we're told not to question authority and to obey our parents and teachers. Fear of being social outcasts makes us avoid saying no to friends. We eventually fall into the habit of saying yes in relationships—sometimes despite our better judgment— because we want to be loved. We need to be mindful of what this translates to. At what cost am I saying yes? Am I saying yes to others and no to being me? Your soul needs to find a balance between yes and no.

Fear is nothing if you don't believe in it. Believing in it is the only power it has. It can't create anything; it can't even exist without you believing it does. Like the boogeyman lurking in the dark under your bed, he exists only so long as you're thinking of him.

As part of the curriculum at a nine-day course I took in Los Angeles a few years ago, we had to go on a daily, early-morning walk. We were divided into small groups, and the exercise was to be done in silence. I noticed a blind woman in my group who always walked arm in arm with someone. I wanted to take part, so at the next opportunity, I asked her if I could walk with her the following morning. She said yes.

Before we started our walk the next morning, I asked her if she needed me to give her directions or describe the terrain. She just said, "No need. If you hesitate, I'll notice, and I'll figure it out."

I was floored by her reply. It made my mind go off on so many tangents, recalling how many times in my life I'd hesitated and not noticed that doing so was robbing me of a positive experience. And here was a blind woman who didn't require any further assistance from a walking buddy than for her to be tuned in and present. She didn't see my tears as I walked silently, but I'm sure she felt them.

People are afraid to see. They're afraid of relationships and of deep intimacy, afraid of their own selves and their inner power and capabilities. They're afraid to see who they truly are. But if you're afraid to see and you look in the mirror, you won't be able to see your own reflection. What will you see instead? What then?

The art of becoming one's own person, of being you, identifying who you really are and the kind of person you want to be, is a job that only you can do. You can seek help, advice, and even allow others to do so much along the way, but it all comes down to you in the end. Only you will decide and know who you want to be. You do it alone, but you don't have to do it in isolation. Self-help is not self-isolation. It's through our relationships and connections with other people that we discover things about ourselves and learning from their experiences helps us learn more about ourselves. People are teachers. Every interaction is a lesson.

Only you can bring down your psychological armor—the walls you build around you to protect yourself and keep out the world. Nobody else can take your armor away or break down these walls for you. You're the one who has to do the work.

People tend to shy away from therapy or coaching. But sometimes you need to talk to someone who'll listen and care without bias or judgment. In 2016, the World Health Organization stated that there were three hundred and fifty million people suffering from depression, and the number of depressed women is higher than that of men only because many cases go unreported. People believe you just have to suck it up and deal with it. Depression is an epidemic that's crippling our societies.

The first step to a solution is to talk about the problem. That means running to the pain—the fear—and facing it. Pulling it out of the darkness and letting the light obliterate it. Running away from your pain and fear will make your emotional issues only pile up like dirty laundry you don't ever get around to washing. Sooner or later, they will stink up everything.

In meditation classes, I tell the participants to sit with their pain. It's hard to grasp this concept at first, but with practice, you learn to become the witness of your emotions and separate from them. You come to see for yourself that *you* aren't your pain. *You* aren't your story. You're a witness who is learning and growing.

The first step is saying, "This is who I am," and knowing it. It's the ground-level work without which nothing can be built and nothing can grow. It starts with "Who do I want to be?" This is where I feel grounded in my intentions, secure in who I am, and comfortable in my own skin and unapologetically being me. This means rooting yourself in your convictions of knowing you can and will, very much like being the roots of a tree and deciding what kind of a tree you want to be. What are the fruits you want to give Earth? Without having that conviction and deliberate intention, we feel lost and unbalanced.

Exercise

Give yourself plenty of time to play with this exercise, and have fun as you describe the part of you that is always fearful or negative. This is your saboteur. Describe that part as much as you can by finding the answers to the following so you can really get familiar with him/her. You may feel resistance doing this, but fight through and stick with it. It is eye-opening when we can dig deep this way.

- name

- favorite stories or things to say over and over again

- preferred times for showing up and how it likes to hi-jack or sabotage your life

- secret fears

- what it would say about its crucial role in your life

Explore your relationship with this dark side of you and how it affects the way you honor your values, your passions, and your relationships with other people.

Chapter 6

The Power of This Moment

As long as you are unable to access the power of the Now, every emotional pain that you experience leaves behind a residue of pain that lives on in you.

—Eckhart Tolle, *The Power of Now: A Guide to Spiritual Enlightenment*

WHEN I first left my ex-husband, a close friend of mine gave me sanctuary in her home. She gave me the space and privacy to wallow in my misery and feel sorry for myself. I stayed in her guest bedroom for days on end. My only companion was Eckhart Tolle's book *The Power of Now: A Guide to Spiritual Enlightenment.*

I couldn't have picked a better book for that period in my life, and I couldn't have learned a better message than what it taught me. Let me share that message with you in a nutshell.

In just about any uncomfortable or stressful situation, there are only three options for what can be done. No matter how you look at it, it will be variations on those three options. Everything comes down to which option you act on now:

- · You can change the situation.

- · You can change yourself.

- · You can remove yourself from the situation.

Any situation can be changed. You can change your circumstances or talk to someone to change their opinion or attitude, come to a mutual agreement of sorts, or fix what is broken; you can find a solution in one form or another. Sometimes, though, you know that's impossible, especially when it involves another person, because you really don't have any control over how they react, respond, or cooperate.

The second option is to change yourself or your thoughts and the way you view the situation. The reality is that the only person you have control over is yourself. You can change your attitude toward someone, you can change your opinion about the circumstances, and you can change just about anything you set your mind to. The first crucial step here is to admit that something in you is what has to change.

If that's not for you, or if you've tried and tried and the situation is still unbearable or stressful, the last option is to remove yourself from it. This is the hardest of the options by far, but it may be the most liberating. This could mean abandoning a friend or ending a marriage or leaving a great school or going to a different country. Very tough to do, and most people are reluctant to change—sometimes to their own detriment. Once that change is made, though, life starts smiling again. You just have to believe it will.

If there's no action you can take, and you are unable to remove yourself from it, then use the situation as a learning tool. Use it to go deeper into surrendering to what is happening and to go deeper into the now—into just being. This is not to say that you need to accept an undesirable situation or to deceive yourself into thinking there's nothing wrong with it. Feeling stuck is an opportunity to narrow down your focus and attention to the present moment without any judgment, negativity, or resistance. And that's exactly when you will be in the most resourceful state of mind to know what else can be done to get out of the unpleasant situation.

I got a firsthand exercise in this lesson during my short-lived marriage. When things started to get tough, I tried unsuccessfully to change him. I wanted to control his diet because he was so skinny and kept on losing weight just by breathing. I wanted to control his schedule because he wasn't spending enough time with me, which made me miserable, and he seemed to spend time with everyone else. I wanted to control our finances because he had so much debt; declaring bankruptcy was on the table.

Trying to change someone else is madness. We can hardly control ourselves, let alone someone else. Think of the last time you were on a diet and a piece of chocolate magically made its way within arm's reach. You battle with the idea of being in control, but you really aren't. At least that's what happens to me with chocolate; my favorite treat is sugar-coated almonds with chocolate dripped on top. But that's another story.

Back to my miserable marriage. I next tried to change myself and the situation. I read books about relationships and marriage. I looked for retreats for couples and found one. We went. It was great. But the benefits lasted as long as Tylenol would for a severe toothache. Within six months of the retreat, which I found truly life-changing, we went back to how things had been, and it was torturous.

I decided to do something alone; I went to a women's retreat. In those four intense days, I made my decision and got all the signs from above that it was the right one. When I went back home, things escalated until I decided to walk out. Before he left for a wedding on a Caribbean island, I told him that by the time he got back, I'd be packed up and gone. He still went to the wedding. I packed up and left.

It was a heart-wrenching week. I cried like I'd never cried before. I cried about the two and a half years of my life I felt I'd wasted. I cried about the unknown future I hadn't planned out yet. I cried over my poor heart, which had told me not to get into this marriage in the first place. I cried because I had defied my parents to marry him and now felt defeated. But I pulled together all the strength in the world and removed myself from a situation I no longer wanted to tolerate. My face burst with acne, and I hid in my friend's guest room for weeks until I was ready to face the world again. I made a choice and took action. I am who I am today because of this experience. I don't wish it on anyone, but sometimes, as in my case, it could be the best thing to ever happen to you.

It's difficult to remember that you're always in control. You're in control of now and what you can do right at this moment about anything at all. And time is your friend, though it can also be your foe. The longer you take to act, the longer time will give you more of whatever it is you want to end, the longer it will make you wait for what you want to have. Time and pain have a pact. So, the choice is yours. Act now!

Acting now was what I did. I gave myself a deadline for my depressed state, and when I hit that deadline, I came out of the guest room ready to take on a new year. I realized how free I was to choose, and that in itself was enough to get me out of my depression. I had met my ex-husband on the dance floor of a Latino nightclub in Toronto. Our marriage was void of any music, and the dancing had stopped. Now, I was free to dance again, and I did.

We have to learn to free ourselves of our negative emotions. We need to disconnect because we aren't our emotions; we only experience them.

According to a seminar I attended for Deepak Chopra called "Soul Leadership," here are the primary negative emotions we need to divorce ourselves from:

- anger and hostility, which are remembered pain from the past

- fear, the anticipation of pain in the future because you didn't learn to deal with it in the past

- guilt, the tendency to direct blame toward yourself when you don't know where else to assign it

· depression, a natural consequence of any or all the above

Stephen R. Covey, an American educator, author, and businessman, says that between every action and response, there's a gap of time, and in it, you have a choice. The gap he's referring to is the now. It's the moment through which all your future will pass. In this moment, you not only have a choice, but you also have a responsibility. You may have suffered despicable injustice, you may have been tortured or bullied by loved ones, or you may be at a loss in your life. They were the cause of your pain; they are to blame, but it's your responsibility how you'll react to what has happened. And nobody has control over that. Nobody but you.

Chapter 7

Diving into Psychology

One who looks outside, dreams.
One who looks inside, awakens.

—Carl Jung

Each of us has the common sense and ability to decipher what's really going on in a particular situation, whether it's an internal dialogue we're having with ourselves or with someone we care about. Yet as was the case with me in my early twenties, I could spot it, identify it, acknowledge it, maybe even understand it, but I sure as hell didn't have the skills to effectively create a change that could help me out of my own cosmic black holes or away from the downward-spiraling, slippery roads of conflict with those closest to me.

Here's a bit of practical psychology for you. There are three essential, basic points, so to speak, to help you understand human beings better:

1. Understanding what stops us from moving forward—fear

2. Understanding what controls our life—the meaning we give to our experiences based on our values and belief systems

3. Understanding what ultimately drives our behavior and makes us do what we do—the six human needs

Why is it important for you to know this? Good question. With understanding, you have more clarity. The more you can understand what's going on with people, the more compassion, connection, and positive influence you can have. Isn't this a super-important skill that any parent, sibling, leader, boss, professional, partner, spouse, or friend should have? I think the answer is yes. As an old adage says, "What lies before us and what lies behind us is nothing compared to what lies within us." So, a bit of Psychology 101 won't hurt anybody.

The first point is to understand what stops us from moving forward, taking action, and being our true selves—fear. Fear stops us in our tracks. And I hope you agree that we beat this point to death already.

The second point is understanding what controls and determines the quality of our life. Tony Robbins says, "Nothing in life has any meaning except the meaning we give it." That's a hard one to swallow. Meanings we associate with the things in our lives shape our psyches and the ways we view the world. Meaning comes from the beliefs and values we've created for ourselves or that we've decided to live by. Meaning affects everything that happens to us and the ways we interpret it.

Two people may experience the same event. One person may think, *God is punishing me. I might as well die.* But the other one might think, *God is challenging me. This is the greatest gift I've ever received.* The difference in how each of those people perceives the event affects not only the quality of their lives, but also what action they will take next. This meaning creates a pattern of emotions that are associated with it as our coping mechanism.

For example, if you were slapped across the face, you may strike back with physical violence. Or you may believe it's important to save face and pretend the attack didn't affect you at all. Or you may respond by trying to hide and protect yourself by avoiding this person or similar situations at all costs. The differences in meanings and the emotions generated by them are virtually limitless.

The third point is understanding why we do what we do, what ultimately drives all human action. How is it that one person will sacrifice his own life for someone else, while another person will commit murder for the thrill of it? What creates a Martin Luther King, Jr. and a suicide bomber? A Margaret Thatcher and a Marilyn Monroe? A Sheikh Zayed bin Sultan Al Nahyan and an Adolf Hitler?

Regardless of who we are—our backgrounds, our professions, our religions, our races—we are driven, day after day, by a common force that shapes all our emotions and actions. This force wants to fulfill the primal needs that have been encoded into our nervous systems over centuries. Although each of us is a unique and special soul, we're all wired the same way.

There are six primal or basic human needs within us, as per the Robbins-Madanes Center for Strategic Intervention:

- Certainty (a.k.a. security, reliability, predictability, comfort zone, or dependability). We want to be comfortable, experience pleasure, and avoid pain. This is when people are very content in their comfort zones and their routines: "This is how I do it, and I like to do it this way, and there's nothing you can tell me that will make me change my mind and do it differently." It's a routine, structure, habit.

- Uncertainty or variety. Whoever said we are simple beings? This obviously creates a paradox in relation to the first need. We want the certainty of knowing we will get our salary at the end of every pay period, but we also want a vacation to run away from the office routine.

- Love and connection. Everyone needs connection with other human beings; everyone strives and hopes for true love. That's why we want to belong to circles, groups, communities, or clubs. We want to blend in. We all want to be valued, to know we're loved, needed, understood. This is why we want to communicate and connect with others around us. No matter what our values or moral code, we'll do whatever it takes to feel we matter to somebody and that we belong. That's why even extreme practices like hazing can be acceptable to some and why others become doormats or people pleasers. We are ready to do anything to meet this need.

· Significance. Yet another paradox, this one in relation to love and connection: I want to blend in, yet I want to stand out. Every person needs to feel special, important, validated, needed, wanted. There's a sense of pride here that needs to be met and acknowledged. "My opinion or work is important. I'm better. I'm different. I want an award. I want to be thanked, appreciated, and acknowledged." If you want a raise or an award, or simply a letter of appreciation, it's to meet this need. Neglect this need, and it turns you into a self-centered egoist. Whenever your ego feels hurt, chances are that your need for significance is not being met. It's similar to the need for love and connection yet different.

The last two are spiritual needs:

· Growth. When we stop growing, we die. We need to develop constantly: emotionally, mentally, physically, and spiritually. We are not here to shrink down but to grow up and blossom into more. We're here to use our time to expand into our full potential so we can play our parts and fulfill our responsibilities in the world.

· Contribution. This is all about the greater good and being of service to the world. This need is about going beyond your own personal desires and reaching out to help others, give to others, and leave an impact. When your dreams and goals include service to others, your accomplishments are accelerated because the universe conspires to help you serve. We want to be part of something bigger than ourselves—to make a difference.

There is no conscious effort required; our will to satisfy these primal needs is automatic. We can use positive channels, neutral channels, or, if necessary, even negative channels to meet these needs. They're like the air we breathe, the food we eat, and the water we drink. We can't choose one and not the others. We need air *and* food *and* water to survive, and it's the same with these six human needs.

While we all have the same needs, we value them in different proportions. We need to meet them in ourselves and in our relationships. For our relationships to succeed, we need to learn what one another's top two needs are and what has to happen for both parties to feel those needs are being fulfilled so we can all go on with our lives and be happy.

Chapter 8

Why Happiness is Good for You

Everybody in the world is seeking happiness—and there is one sure way to find it. That is by controlling your thoughts. Happiness doesn't depend on outward conditions. It depends on inner conditions. It isn't what you have or who you are or what you are doing that makes you happy or unhappy. It is what you think about it.

—Dale Carnegie, How to Win Friends and Influence People: The Only Book You Need to Lead You to Success

Psychologists working in the field of positive psychology report that we are moderately happy most of the time. In my workshops, I ask people to rate their overall happiness level in life on a scale of one to ten, where one is sad and ten is happy, and the majority would say seven to eight. Or so they think. Nowadays, experts constantly insist that we think positively. Doctors tell us to manage our stress and depression to improve our health, reduce the risk of a stroke, and help us to live longer. Executive coaches advise us that happy, optimistic employees earn more money and climb the career ladder faster. Positive psychology researchers publish studies showing that optimistic people are happier and have more friends. Somehow, we have to paste that smile on our face to get the world's approval, and those of us who are unhappy or even depressed are left to mope in the dark, separated from those happy people.

According to a prediction by the World Health Organization, by 2020, depression will be second only to heart disease in terms of the global burden of illness. David Lester, an American psychology professor, knows more about suicide than anyone else. He has twenty-five hundred academic publications in which he has explored suicide and its relationship to alcohol, antidepressants, blood type, IQ, drugs, TV, vacation time, and everything else you can imagine in depth. He has concluded that suicide is more common among people with a higher quality of life, simply because they have no external reason to blame for their unhappiness. Those who are less fortunate, on the other hand, are more immune to suicide because they have ample excuses for their perceived or real misery.

At the University of Minnesota, Dr. David Lykken tried to explain how we go to our "happiness set point," very much like the thermostat setting of your air conditioner or furnace. We each have a set point—our default level of happiness—which we always revert to, whether it's genetic or conditioned or learned. His studies found that 50 percent of that happiness set point is genetic; 10 percent is determined by outside factors like level of wealth, marital status, and career success; and 40 percent comes from habitual thoughts and feelings, the words we use, and the actions we take[4].

In the book *Happy for No Reason: 7 Steps to Being Happy from the Inside Out*, Marci Shimoff and Carol Kline explain how research shows that no matter what happens to you in life—positive or negative—your set point will peak or dip for a while, but it will always return to its predetermined spot. One study tracked the happiness life span of people who won the lottery. Within six to twelve months, they resumed their typical set point after a spike in their happiness level. Likewise, when they tracked people who had become paraplegic or contracted cancer, within six to twelve months, their diminished happiness returned to their normal set point. Research further showed that the only three exceptions to this are when a person suffers from the loss of a spouse, chronic unemployment, or extreme poverty, which takes longer to recover from.

The good news is that we can change that set point simply by changing our thoughts, which trigger feelings and actions.

I attended a most interesting talk in Abu Dhabi a few years back by Shawn Achor, who spent over a decade at Harvard University working on positive psychology research and won over a dozen distinguished teaching awards for his efforts. Here's his list of the advantages of just being a happy person at work. Not that we really need to be convinced it's good to be happy; this is for the skeptics out there—you know who you are.

· You will become 3 times more creative.

- You will become 31 percent more productive.

- You will have 37 percent more sales.

- You will be 40 percent more likely to receive a promotion.

- You will end up with 23 percent fewer fatigue symptoms.

- You will have up to 10 times more energy.

- You will be 39 percent more likely to live to ninety-four[5].

I said it before, and I'll say it again: happy people change the world. With that elevated happiness level, you'll have more energy, and with more energy, you'll be more creative and productive in whatever you do.

Achor's research also showed that IQ predicts 25 percent of success in a job or a job interview, and people's optimism level, social support, and ability to see stress as a challenge instead of a threat predict 75 percent of that success. In other words, your success is more about how you feel than about what you know. How many people do you know who are super smart at something, yet they haven't a clue how to interact with others or keep their anal perfectionism in check or manage their emotions? The quality of your life is directly proportionate to the quality of your emotions. It's 25 percent mechanics—what you know—and 75 percent psychology—your mind-set. Emotional intelligence is more important than intellectual intelligence. I wish more parents would wake up to this fact and make it part of their parenting style and pay attention to their kids' feelings as much as they worry about their academic performance.

Our brain has an advantage when it's happy, according to Achor. We have what are called mirror neurons, which pick up on negativity from other people. To give you an example, you walk into an elevator feeling particularly energetic or happy that day. You say good morning to the other person in there, and he doesn't reply. Leaving the elevator, something has latched on to you; his expressionless face is in your mind, and depending on how emotionally strong you are, your happiness level is affected.

Too many studies and social experiments to mention have proven that integrating the following as regular habits significantly increases your overall sense of satisfaction with your life:

- journaling

- exercise

- random acts of kindness

- gratitude lists

- meditation

How much simpler can it get? So, let's get on with it, people. Let's create a wave of happiness to crush the negativity around us at home, in the office, even when stuck in a traffic jam or on an elevator with Mr. Poker Face. It's a matter of choice, really. Choose to be happy when you first wake up in the morning. Choose to be happy every day. It's like choosing to have a healthy lifestyle. It comes down to what you do on a regular basis. The little things you do in your day-to-day become the big results you achieve in your lifetime.

The brain is the last organ to become anatomically mature, taking all our first twenty years of life to finish growing. And just as with a plant, the quality of the soil and fertilizer you use, whether it's rich or depleted, impacts that growth. A child's brain will shape itself to match the social and emotional environment it grows up in. Experiments show that a depressed mother who engages less with her baby is more likely to have a child who is less able to self-soothe and less efficient at human interactions than one with a totally engaged mother. Some basic emotions like fear and joy are hardwired in us, but others, like empathy, require a self-consciousness that starts at around two years of age. So the social relationships we have at that stage and the emotional stability of a child's home are of the utmost importance in determining the emotional intelligence of the adult she will become. Awareness of all this can be the start of a major shift in your life today, no matter what kind of childhood you had.

You're in charge of your happiness. Nobody has that control over you without your permission. If you don't like something, change it. If it's something you can't change, then change the way you view it or your attitude toward it. But whatever you do, don't just complain, and don't sit there as if you're helpless to make a change.

You need three things to ensure you're among those who succeed at whatever they set their minds to, including becoming happy, no matter what:

1. Commitment - Decide to be part of your own solution, not part of the problem.

2. Control - Keep a sense of resolve instead of resignation. Feel and know that you have what it takes and that you aren't the victim of your circumstances.

3. Challenge - Use whatever crisis you're in to strengthen yourself and build your muscles of resilience and perseverance. Only the disciplined are free. The undisciplined are slaves to their moods and emotions.

Don't give control over your emotions to anyone else. It's like giving the remote control of your air conditioner or your television to the neighbors! Who would do that?

I wrote the next few pages with caution for fear of giving the pessimists out there an excuse to continue wrecking the world with their moods. The interesting thing about people who engage in defensive pessimism is that they tend to be quite dynamic and successful. They use their pessimism as a motivator to do better—to be the best at what they do. Just like any negative emotion, if pessimism is used to keep you moving forward in a constructive manner, then so be it.

Negative emotions don't necessarily mean bad news. They aren't all created equal. Evolution has equipped us with a myriad of emotions, including jealousy, envy, fear, rage, joy, humiliation, passion, and love. To understand on a deeper level the mechanism of these feelings wouldn't necessarily help us avoid the negative ones, but at least it would help by giving us the emotional intelligence and wisdom to deal with this ocean of emotions.

In his book *Flourish: A Visionary New Understanding of Happiness and Well-Being*, American psychologist Martin E. P. Seligman explains his pioneering experiments in the 1970s, which showed the ultimate negative mind-set—depression—was largely a consequence of learned helplessness. The opposite of this passive, defeated state is learned happiness—the gateway to optimal functioning.

He said that the idea that optimism is always good is not realistic because it discounts the importance of negative emotions—such as pessimism—in our life. An advocate of optimism, Seligman says it must be paired with "reality testing": conscientious checking on the results of our efforts to make sure overly positive expectations aren't leading us astray.

Pessimism can sometimes be an ally. As he explains in his book, the elderly people who are realistic and even pessimistic about the likelihood of experiencing negative life events are actually less vulnerable to depression than the more optimistic ones. In this case, that dose of pessimism offers protection against the pain of loss or grief.

In Seligman's view, life has four parts, and only one of them is positive emotion. The other three parts are engagement with what one's doing, a sense of accomplishment, and good relationships. This book covers all these parts.

Happiness does have a self-fulfilling aspect to it. In many situations, positive expectations lead to positive outcomes. What you focus on expands in your life. It's as if you have antennae tuned into the thing you focus on, therefore attracting more of it to your path. It's the law of attraction at work.

Part III

Butterflies

When you are inspired by some great purpose, some extraordinary project, all your thoughts break their bonds. Your mind transcends limitations, your consciousness expands in every direction, and you find yourself in a new, great, and wonderful world.

—Patañjali, *The Yoga Sutras of Patañjali*

Chapter 9

The Well-Being of Your Heart, Mind, Body, and Soul

One man cannot do right in one department of life whilst he is occupied in doing wrong in any other department. Life is one indivisible whole.

—Mahatma Gandhi

STRIPPING it to the bare essentials, the down-to-earth basics, happiness and a life of fulfillment and well-being can be achieved by honoring the elements that make up the human in human beings. Just as fire, water, earth, and air are the four elements of life, the heart, mind, body, and soul are the four elements of a human being. Any disrespect, negligence, or dishonoring of any of those elements will create an imbalance.

Nature is all about balance. The more you're in tune with your being, the more alert and aware you will be of any imbalance. You'll know you're out of balance when symptoms occur. Symptoms like depression, dissatisfaction, stress, emotional turmoil, sadness, negativity, anger, shortness of breath, feeling there's not enough time, feeling overwhelmed. The list goes on and on …

Choosing to be happy is like choosing to have a healthy lifestyle. It takes time, but it also takes emotional intelligence because that twelve-inch distance between the heart and the brain makes all the difference. It's not a secret that if you want to be healthier or you want to lose weight, all you have to do is exercise more and eat less. Yet what do we have? We have an obesity and diabetes epidemic, even though the solution is there for anyone who wants to lose weight to apply. What's missing is the emotional intelligence. Emotional intelligence is what triggers action, and it's the same with being happy.

The quality of your emotions has a direct consequence on the quality of your life and your personal and professional success. Emotional intelligence starts with taking responsibility for your emotions.

But what exactly is emotional intelligence? I'll explain it in the simplest way possible because many people I discuss it with are actually confused or clueless about what it really means to be an emotionally intelligent person. To be so, you need to have all the following:

- self-awareness - knowing your own emotional tendencies

- self-regulation - managing your emotions for positive outcomes

- motivation - maintaining a passion and commitment to your goals

- empathy - sincere belief in the validity of other people's emotions and accepting them as legitimate

- social skills - the ability to apply this intelligence to create a favorable interaction in order to win allies, resolve conflicts, and work together

How do you practice emotional intelligence and increase it? Here are five steps that I promise will help you immensely if you wholeheartedly and mindfully commit to them whenever you have an emotional "tantrum" of sorts:

1. Become aware of your emotions on a regular basis, especially when they are stirred up in an unfavorable way, and of the emotions of any person you are having an issue with. Meditation will help you with this immensely. You need to be able to identify that emotion when it surfaces so you can understand what's behind that state or mood you are in. You need to dig a little deeper, like peeling an onion one layer at a time. You can't just do the typical thing of blowing it off by saying, "I'm fine," or "It's nothing." Dig deep. Be curious.

2. Recognize the emotion as an opportunity for learning and improving your relationship with yourself or the person who triggered the emotion. Acknowledge that this is an opportunity to learn and teach.

3. You need to listen empathetically and validate the other's emotions (or your emotions if no other person is involved). It is most important to really use all your

listening skills here. Do not just listen for the words but for the emotion and the feeling behind them. No matter what it is, you need to first *validate* the emotion before you even start to fix the problem. You need to get curious and allow self-expression. Your job is to absorb and understand.

4. Find words to label the emotion you are having or that the other person is having. This is a major coaching skill we are taught as life coaches. At the beginning of every session, I ask my client, "What do you want coaching on?" and I need to clarify until it is clear what she wants. We need to learn how to express and verbalize our emotions better.

5. STOP, which stands for Stop and Think Of Possibilities, while exploring options and strategies to solve the problem at hand. Stephen R. Covey said that between every action and reaction, there is that split second, that gap of time in which we get to decide how we will react[6]. I invite you to stretch that gap long enough so that when you do take action, it will come from an empowered and resourceful state of mind.

Taking care of your well-being comes down to daily commitments you choose to integrate that become your lifestyle —your way of living. Remember, everything is a choice. This is about what you choose to make part of your daily life —a new, exciting routine—at the office, at home, and even between yourself and the mirror. And until you commit to having this new lifestyle, nothing will change. Without energy, without excitement, without passion, nothing changes.

Carve out time in your day to nurture these elements, and you're on your way to a happier you in no time at all. Find out what it is that would fulfill your needs, and create your own formula. This is time for maintenance that you'll carve out for yourself. I call it "me time." Stephen Covey calls it "sharpening the saw." Make it work for you. It can be a morning or evening ritual, or it can be little chunks of time throughout the day or week until you get to the point where it's your way of life. Find an easy starting point for you, and work your way up from there. Commit to something that's nonnegotiable going forward.

In my private Facebook group, we start every month with a five-day challenge; everyone picks their own thing they want to commit to that will help them live better. They have to publicly share what that is because there's so much power when you know you're being held accountable. Robert B. Cialdini says that people are way more committed to their word when it is said publicly and even more so when it is written down. In his amazing book *Influence: The Psychology of Persuasion*, he describes many social psychology experiments and studies proving that going public about something, even if it is as simple a thing as stating one's opinion, makes the person more stubborn about that opinion, even if more evidence is shown to prove the opinion is wrong. The secret sauce is that people want to be consistent with the image they portray to the outside world and, therefore, will be more committed to that image. Your commitment shouldn't be a secret. The advantage of the group is that you get support from like-minded people committed to their own challenges. That's how we lift one another up.

Whenever I feel stressed out, I immediately know I'm ignoring my me time. I let everything else take priority over taking care of myself. I eventually have a meltdown. Over the years, while in the process of writing this book, I reached that point many times. Every year, I resort to the best recovery treatment, and I travel somewhere. The book comes along. I'm spending a month in Sri Lanka as I write this part. This book traveled with me to Belize, Ireland, Canada, Spain, Thailand, and India while it was still in the making. This was my way of honoring myself and addressing the needs of my heart, mind, body, and soul.

While here in Sri Lanka, I'm doing a yoga retreat for a week, followed by another week of surfing, and finishing off with two weeks at an ayurvedic healing resort. It's the ideal vacation, but the idea is to have a road map where I feel as if I'm on vacation even when I'm at home or at work. It's very easy to meditate when you isolate yourself by going into a cave, but the true challenge is practicing meditation in the hub of the city, where life is coming at you from every angle.

God created us free and gave us a little secret gift. Like a seed with the potential to grow into a mighty cedar tree, we are born. And every day, we have a new pack of energy we have to spend emotionally, mentally, physically, and spiritually. That's why it's super important to manage our emotions. The quality of our life is equal to the quality of our emotions. Negative emotions drain us because they have low vibrational energies and leave us with little to keep going along the path to being our true selves. Once we discover our secret gift, our life mission, the world conspires to help us unleash it.

The heart wants to love. Love is everything; it's the fertile soil for relationships. The mind wants to create, to unleash the creator within you. Try sitting still and noticing what's going on inside your head. A million and one thoughts— let's make them constructive. Your body wants to grow. If we aren't growing, we're dying. Rejuvenation is the key. Your soul wants to serve. It wants to leave a legacy in service of the greater good of the world. And what better way than by doing what you love to do most? We're born with a talent. God wants to see you exercising your full potential and enjoying yourself along the way. That's the meaning of life: to live a life of meaning.

Exercise

For two hours, simply be with yourself. (Notice your reactions to this assignment, and observe those reactions too.) Explore what simply being means for you. Note any temptation to do something or to fit this exercise into something you already know, like journaling, meditating, or even reflecting, and bring your attention back to simply being.

Chapter 10

Your Heart Wants to Love

Your task is not to seek for love, but merely to seek and find all the barriers within yourself that you have built against it.

—Rumi

We all emit an energy wave. From quantum physics, we know that waves vibrate. This energy intelligence is a form of communication. To change your relationships, you need to be conscious of and responsible for your own energy, and you also need to be able to read the energy from anyone you're trying to connect with.

Think about this: we make our decisions based on vibes. We gravitate to those people and things and places that make us feel good. The more sensitive you are to these environmental vibrations, the more intuitive you are. This is emotional intelligence. The ability to read other people's energy comes through our heart. The more you are in tune with your own feelings and heart, the better you are at reading other people.

So, what does the heart want? To love. Why love? Why this temporary insanity that drives people to do the weirdest things, distracts them from work, causes loss of appetite, and fills their minds with obsessive thoughts? It's because love itself evolved to resolve issues of commitment and abandonment. It's the solution to being lonely or abandoned.

The heart is where it's all at. One can be brain-dead and in a coma but still alive. When the heart is dead, though, it's game over.

Your heart contains so much love and passion by default. It keeps beating for you unconditionally. In my workshops and private coaching practice, I often ask, "When was the last time you spoke to your heart?" I get a blank expression on the faces of participants 95 percent of the time, followed by the question, "What do you mean exactly by talking to my heart?" Just say hello. Just sit quietly until you feel your heartbeats. Even if you never talk to it or check in with it, your heart loves you unconditionally. However, like fire, it can consume you, devouring everything that comes its way because that's what it does. It's meant to give openly and generously to create warmth for you and anyone who's in touch with you. It even goes well beyond that circle of loved ones and people you care about. It extends to strangers and anyone or anything you empathize with.

Love is a flame that cleanses but does not burn. Like a flame, it appears to be one continuous body but is actually constantly and forever changing in form and shape. You can never love two people in exactly the same way. You can't love the same person the same way every day. Ever changing, ever growing, the love you share with the world is infinite. But you need to honor your heart.

You need to start by loving yourself. If you look in the mirror and can't say, "I love you," to yourself, then why would you expect another person to do so? How do you suppose you'll attract love when you don't even give it to yourself? You need to send out a vibe that says, "I'm someone who loves herself, and you can love me, too!" Or "I love me as is, and I welcome love with open arms." Find your own words, your own mantra to live by. You are responsible for the vibes you give off.

You have to love yourself first. You don't need another person to be complete. You fill the void you feel. It's nobody else's job. If you want to change how others treat you, you should change the way you treat yourself. Unless you truly love yourself, you can't be loved.

Love is mindful, present, and deliberate. Relationships come and go, but love remains. It just changes form. Every true love or friendship or relationship is a story of unexpected transformation. If you're the exact same person before and after the relationship, you haven't loved enough. Love is the only truth. Everything else is just stories. "Divorce your stories, and marry the truth," I tell the women at my retreats, and I stand witness to how they start embracing life from a new and much kinder perspective now that they can love themselves enough first. I witness caterpillars turning into chrysalises turning into butterflies.

It's the underlying missing ingredient for almost every person who comes to me for life coaching. People go about their lives as if love is scarce, when in reality, it's so abundant, it's everywhere. The signs are everywhere, but we refuse to see them. The messages are everywhere, but we refuse to listen. You can deny, argue, disagree, bitch, and moan about it. You can accuse me of patronizing you with all the love talk when the world around us is full of hatred. I know that just one scroll down my Facebook wall is enough to depress anyone nowadays. But what you focus on expands. I say, "If you don't like it, change it. It starts right here, right now." It starts with me. It starts with you.

How much do you love yourself? How much do you love your every day? How much do you love your reflection in the mirror or the fat on your thighs? The body you live with? The work you do? The sky in the morning, just because?

Up the dose. Turn up the love. Don't say you can't or you don't know how. I challenge you. You can. Just consciously notice every little love-ly thing around you … and then amplify it. Decide you will be the source of it.

We behave differently when our love tank is full instead of empty. A tank check is in order on a regular basis.

Here's the thing: we suffer only when we lose things or lose people, but when they're still around, we have no capacity for recognizing them as precious. You are precious!

Each and every one of us has the capacity to love beyond belief. It literally runs through our veins and is infinite. There's so much of it to go around for everybody and everything. Yet we hold back. We tell ourselves lies. We don't want to be seen as vulnerable and imperfect. Well, let me tell you, that's a load of horse crap. And it's exactly that crap that makes people treat one another like garbage because we treat ourselves like garbage, feeding our own minds with crap that's not true. That's why people go to war, kill one another, abuse animals, and pollute our planet. Enough!

In the early 1980s, there was a wake-up call. We realized heart attacks killed more women than men, more women of all age groups than breast cancer. You don't get any goodbyes or any notice. This is all because of stress, which comes from our thoughts and our choices on a daily basis, what we believe, and how we act.

All we need is love—start by giving it. *Love* is a verb, too, you know. It's something you do. Do love. You can choose love, or you can choose fear. I choose love. I choose love again and again and again.

Choose love. Change your life. Inspire others to do the same. Show your kids there's another way. Transform the world.

Without mindfulness, you allow your senses and emotions to take over and run your life, ruining this very moment by reacting to them rather than refraining. We become poisoned. Intoxicated. We suffer innumerable times and from many negative emotions like anger, hatred, jealousy, and despair. We choose to torture ourselves day and night.

In order to restore love, we need to communicate more. It's sad how within one family, many members don't even look at one another. Distractions like TV, the internet, and chores are all more important than having a human, heart-to-heart connection.

We need to start listening again for no other purpose but to understand and maybe help others suffer less. Allow them time to speak, express, and therefore heal. We process two hundred and twenty-five words per minute when we talk and five hundred when we listen. Don't react; just listen, even if you think what they're saying is crap. It's their time to heal. After a while, it will be your turn to speak, with kindness and compassion because you now understand their pain since you took the time to listen. We prefer to shut down, go to our room, and cry alone rather than speak up and tell others about our pain.

We have a listening problem. And we have a communication problem. In real estate, it's all about location, location, location. In relationships, it's all about communication, communication, communication.

"I did it out of love"—this is given as an explanation for so many behaviors. A politician committing adultery calls it love; the preacher calls it sin. The parent indulges all a child's wishes out of love; the family therapist calls it irresponsible parenting.

Clarity and communication in relationships are important. Constantly ask yourself what is the one thing you can do that would have a significant effect on the quality of your relationship. Then confirm your answer with your partner. Relationships are like ballroom dancing. The very first time I saw two people dance the tango was at a nightclub in Beirut. I was mesmerized. The flow, the connection, the unspoken understanding all played a part in making the man be the strong frame for the woman to float within, and together they were a piece of art more beautiful than anything I'd seen. I've been in love with ballroom dancing ever since.

We each have different ways or languages of giving and receiving love. If we speak only our primary language and meet someone who speaks only his or her own primary language, our communication will be limited—awkward. If we want proper communication, we have to learn other languages, especially those of the ones with whom we want to communicate. In his book *The 5 Love Languages: The Secret to Love That Lasts*, Gary Chapman, a renowned marriage counselor, explains how important it is to first know your own primary love language, then that of your partner or loved ones, so you can effectively communicate and deal with them. How else can you express your love in a way that they will receive it, which makes them feel truly loved? This applies not only to couples but also to relationships with your parents, siblings, and friends.

Dr. Dorothy Tennor did extensive studies on the phenomenon of being in love, and she found that the average span of a romantic obsession is two years. True love starts only after that in-love stage. What we do before marriage is no indication of how we will behave after we wed. During marriage, we revert to the people we were before the in-love stage. The little traits we had ignored become mountains. No two people fall in love at the same time, and no two people fall out of love on the same day. Does that not explain all the pain you hear in country western love songs?

The five love languages are:

- acts of service

- gifts

- words of affirmation

- quality time

- touch

Let's dive deeper into each.

Acts of Service

People with this primary love language express it by doing things for others. They feel most loved when others do things for them. Examples could include anything from washing the dishes, serving breakfast, and running errands to cooking a surprise meal.

Do something you think he/she would appreciate. By simply helping them out, you'll make them feel you truly care and understand them.

If this is your love language and you want your partner to do something for you, request it. A request introduces the element of choice. A demand stops the flow of love. You can request all you want, but never demand. Love is freely given. A request is something your mate may choose to respond to or deny because love is a choice; that's what makes it meaningful.

Gifts

Not to be mistaken for materialism, this love language makes people feel loved when they're remembered at the most unexpected moment. A good example is when you're at the coffee shop and buy them their favorite type of coffee just because it reminded you of them. It's all about the thoughtfulness, love, and effort behind the gift. One good tip for showing them how much you love them? Be attentive when they say they like something, and take note. Give them simple presents that let them know you're always thinking of them.

I love receiving letters and postcards in the mail, so I asked a friend of mine to send me a postcard last time he went on a trip. For whatever reason, he didn't manage to do it, saying it was too complicated to find stamps and a mailbox. The second time he returned from another trip, he put a postcard in my hand and said, "There! I made sure it arrived this time!" I felt loved.

Words of Affirmation

Sometimes, words can speak louder than actions. Think of a time when words—a handwritten letter or text message —had a profound impact on you, making you feel ever so loved, and you went on for weeks telling your close friend about it. If this is your primary love language, compliments, feedback, and encouragement mean the world to you. Hearing the words *I love you* is really important to you, as well as hearing the reasons behind that love. On the contrary, insults, criticisms, and negative comments are especially hurtful to people whose primary language is words. Words and language cause people to misunderstand and misjudge. That's what causes wars and hatred in the world.

If your loved one's love language is words of affirmation, make sure they know how you truly feel. But also make sure you become an expert at listening. Chances are people who speak this language are very talkative and want to express to the moon and back, so listen.

Research shows that the average individual listens for seventeen seconds before interrupting. Just listening without saying a single word is powerful in making others feel heard and therefore loved. In my coaching practice, I don't need to add my story or say words of sympathy or agree or nod my head. Just being present is all I need to be with my clients. Listen in every sense of the word. Allow the words to be uttered uninterrupted. Listen to the feelings in their words. Ask what emotion your partner is experiencing. Then confirm what you heard. Get clear. Communicate.

For example, do you ever think, *I know what they actually mean?* Then you're in your own head with your own story. Do you think, *I know better,* and start giving advice when all they want is to vent? Do you interrupt with something you think is more important than listening?

Notice when you fall into interpretations of the stories you hear. Our interpretations and conclusions taint and hinder communication. Catch yourself when you want to finish a sentence for someone out loud or in your mind.

Quality Time

People who have this as their primary love language feel the most loved when you are fully present and engaging with them. They associate love with your full and undivided attention. Being there for them, especially when they need you the most, is so important. When I give you my time, I never get that back, so it's a strong expression and a powerful communicator of love.

The essential ingredients of what constitutes a quality-time activity are that one of you wants to do it or suggests it, the other is willing, and you both know why you're doing it: it's for love.

It can be really hurtful for these type of people when you fail to listen, postpone a plan, or don't fully focus on them. If your loved one speaks this language, be attentive and ask them what they truly enjoy doing. Set up a date, and make sure to be really present in that moment. Avoid any distractions so you can truly enjoy your quality time together.

When we love someone, love comes in a package along with fear. Fear of separation from that someone. We've forgotten we've survived our lives so far without that person and that we can manage alone again, so we come across as needy. Who's ever attracted to that? Don't be that person.

Physical Touch

A person whose primary love language is physical touch is naturally very touchy-feely. It doesn't mean they have to be all over another person. Such simple gestures as hugging, holding hands, and patting on the back are some of the ways to show how much you love them. Even being touched by the voice of a loved one over the phone has proven to cause a drop in cortisol and have a calming effect[7].

For these people, loving acts like putting your arm around their shoulders, holding their hand while sitting together, or hugging them tightly when they feel low are the ways they feel most loved.

Touch is a very important part of being human. We're saying, "I love you," when we stroke the hair of a little kid or pat them on the head. We're saying, "I love you," when we give a bear hug—my favorite. To communicate love, it can be full-blown sex, and it can just be spooning while watching TV.

We yearn to be touched. We seek it in relationships or casual encounters. We expect it from family and pay for it if it can't be attained any other way. Even in our verbal language, there's so much touching going on: "He captured his audience." "Her story was gripping. It touched my heart." "His words reached out to me."

Babies who are hugged, kissed, and cuddled develop a healthier emotional life than those left for long periods without physical contact. A baby in her mother's womb is in a warm, comfortable, snugly place where she's getting all she needs and wanting for nothing. Then she has to go through birth, which is, come to think of it, the most devastating thing a baby can experience. From the womb to this big cold world is a shock, to say the least. That's why you usually find babies wrapped in blankets. We try to simulate the feeling of being in the womb, surrounded by warmth.

We live in a touch-deprived world. To do my little part to fix that, as a matter of fact, I often get women at my retreats and participants at my workshops to get up and get as many hugs as they can. I explain that it's a different kind of hug. They each need to raise their left arm, then go in for a hug that's six seconds long. With the left arm raised, the embrace is heart to heart, the best kind. No tapping on the back. No need to say anything. Just be. Sometimes there's laughter, our way of camouflaging our emotions and not being present with what's really happening in that moment. Initially, there will be hesitation to get up and do it, but once started, it's almost always a struggle to get them back in their seats to continue the workshop. I always enjoy the feedback I get afterward. I ask if they feel a little more love is present in the room, and the answer is always a resounding yes. The one comment I hear often is that they can't believe how much love they've just received from total strangers.

I also get some who simply won't participate and walk up to me to explain that they got the point of the exercise but don't feel they need to hug strangers to get love, that they're fine as they are, said with arms crossed and the walls visibly up all around them. Sometimes I just nod, and sometimes I give them a hug, interrupting their elaborate explanation.

When I gave this exercise to the sixty officers I mentioned earlier in this book, I suggested they make it a policy in their respective government entities. I invite you to do the same in your own office or home. Whenever someone walks in and their mood is off, ask them how many hugs they received that day. Most probably, it was none or maybe one. Make them go out to get some hugs and then come back to you.

Hugs change and shift your energy higher. When your vibrational energy is high, so is your ability to take risks, to learn, to love, to change, and to heal and grow.

Psychotherapist Virginia Satir famously said, "We need four hugs a day for survival. We need eight hugs a day for maintenance. We need twelve hugs a day for growth." Here's a list of benefits you get simply by hugging.

- A six-second hug increases levels of oxytocin, which is a hormone secreted by the posterior lobe of the pituitary gland at the base of the brain. It is nicknamed "the love hormone" and is beneficial for decreasing stress levels. It's a star in the world of neuroscience because it has been found to make our brains geared for attachment and trust. It gets secreted in our bloodstream when we form and maintain meaningful relationships. This is the same hormone that's secreted whenever we do any act that reflects self-love, like shopping or getting ready for a date. This hormone is constantly battling with cortisol, "the stress hormone."

- A ten-second hug a day may fight infections, boost your immune system, ease depression, and lessen fatigue.

- A twenty-second hug reduces the harmful physical effects of stress, including its impact on your blood pressure and heart rate.

Both the giver and the receiver get just as much benefit, but some research suggests the healthiest hugs come from someone you trust as opposed to a stranger. This applies even when hugging a pet!

So, what's your love language? If you still haven't figured it out, ask yourself the following questions:

1. What do I request of or nag my partner about the most?

2. How do I regularly express love to others?

If you're single, your picture of the perfect partner and what you want him to do and say and how you want him to treat you gives you a very good idea of what your love language is. Remember, we all want to be loved. And we want to be loved through all the languages, but there's always one that's primary, one that we want above all others.

Here's how you can find out what someone else's love language is. It doesn't have to be a partner; it can be a friend or family member or anyone to whom you want to communicate love.

Ask them to remember a specific time when they felt totally, completely, and deeply loved. Then try to discover which triggers caused that magical feeling. Ask them what was absolutely necessary to be there for them to feel loved. Was it being taken places? Did they receive a present? Were they touched or looked at a certain way? Did they hear certain words? Were they treated to something special or a surprise?

By reading their body language, you can tell what excites them the most, and they can show and tell you how much they need any or all the above. Then you can tell which of the love languages they're actually referring to through their story. Always ask, "What do you want?" and when they reply, say, "I hear you," and make them feel heard.

Relationships: The Good, the Bad, and the Ugly

But I tell you who hear: love your enemies, do good to those who hate you, bless those who curse you, and pray for those who mistreat you … And as you would like people to do to you, do the same to them. If you love those who love you, what credit is that to you? For even sinners love those who love them.

—Jesus Christ, Luke 6:27–28, 31–32, *New Heart English Bible*

Relationship stages with a partner are a reflection of our relationship with our parents. During infancy, a baby is totally dependent on her parents for everything: food, warmth, getting cleaned up, etcetera. All she needs to do is cry or be cute, and she gets what she wants. The message she conveys is, "Don't ever leave me."

As a toddler, she wants to explore her surroundings. She's less attached to her mother and wants to venture out on her own to see what's there. She knows Mom is always close by if things get tough. The message now becomes, "Give me space; leave me alone."

As a teen, things change again. She wants to be her own person, choose her own clothes. Interference from her mother isn't welcome anymore. Goodbye kisses as she's dropped off at school are no longer cool. The message now is, "Don't come close to me."

Soon enough, that baby is an adult and on her own. The world feels big, spacious, maybe cold and lonely. With her parents out of the picture, now she will seek relationships that in some way duplicate the stages she experienced with them. On the subconscious level, she may even attract a man who has similar qualities to either or both of her parents.

At the beginning of a relationship, the couple is madly in love and inseparable. Having sex or being intimate is a daily activity. The unspoken message is, "I can't live without you; don't ever leave me."

Once this stage wears off, she may feel as if she needs some time alone or a weekend with her girlfriends. The togetherness starts to suffocate her, and the message to her partner is, "Give me space; leave me alone."

If the relationship continues, they move in together or get married. The sex becomes infrequent. With all the merging of free time, activities, friends, and vacations, her personal identity starts to blur into the marriage identity, and in a panic, she eventually gets to a point where the message she sends her partner is, "Get away from me. Don't touch me; I've gotta leave."

If she does leave, the search to find that special someone who will make up for the intimacy that she needs and craves starts all over again. For some, the cycle is repeated indefinitely. It's all about finding someone who will meet your needs.

Child psychologists affirm that every child has certain basic emotional needs that must be met for a child to become emotionally stable, or this child will grow to become socially and emotionally challenged. Love is one of them. Security, self-worth, and significance are also needed, but love is the common denominator.

We can spend a lifetime searching for significance, self-worth, and security if we don't feel love and may never find them. But when we're loved, there's a higher purpose; life has meaning. Love enables all other basic needs to be met.

We lose the freedom to self-express as children. We ask for something and get a no, so we feel guilty or frustrated or angry. We are scolded, and we slowly dare not express again. By the time we're adults, we're emotionally on mute. How do we ask for love then?

There are three types of relationships. Some last for a short while, having little impact on you. Others last longer and are meant for the other person to teach you a lesson you need to learn. And others last a lifetime. That's where the other person in the relationship is your teacher, with unlimited opportunities for growth for both of you. Yet the most important relationship, and the longest ever, is the one you have with yourself. So every time you see yourself in the mirror, greet yourself and celebrate. Be as excited as you are when you see your best friend!

I am amazed by how many people, and I'm no exception, mess up a new day with yesterday. We're human beings who exercise our right to choose, but sometimes we make horrible choices. We've done hurtful things and uttered poisonous words to one another, and we can't erase the past, but we can say we were wrong and ask for forgiveness and act differently going forward. Love is always a choice, which is why it's meaningful. True love doesn't keep score and bring up past failures. If you kick a dog, it will remember five years later, but it won't spend those five years planning revenge.

Anger comes from wanting to defend and to be fair and to fight for justice. In relationships, it's all about being fair, right? But even if you get the apology when you're used to blame and pointing fingers, that apology won't be enough. It won't heal or transform you.

We have the option of seeking justice or seeking forgiveness. Forgiveness is for you, not for the person who hurt you. It's the secret formula to letting go of grudges. Forgiveness can lower blood pressure and heart rate, as well as reduce depression, anxiety, and anger. Oprah Winfrey said, "Forgiveness is letting go of the hope that the past can be changed."

You want to forgive people so you can stop hurting yourself. Resentment hurts you more that it hurts them. If you aren't in love, you're in fear. These two emotions are the motivators of all our actions and thoughts.

Every argument we have is about love. We're just stuck in the argument because we don't know how to communicate the love through.

There are different levels of love. The most superficial is when you demand it. You bully your partner into loving you. You can con, manipulate, and use shady tactics to win someone over, but it will be at the price of your long-term happiness and peace of mind.

The next level is trading it: I'll love you if you love me back. This is exhausting because you're constantly keeping records; you'll have to hire a bookkeeper! It's not genuine.

The next level is giving it because that's who you are. That's when you're true to your heart. All the heart wants is to love. And if you take that a step further, you give it unconditionally, meaning without expecting anything in return, loving for the sake of it.

A few years ago, I gave a workshop called "Energy Suckers and Emotional Vampires." Needless to say, it was very popular. Don't we all have a few of these people in our lives? But then I added a sudden twist toward the end and got the participants to see when they are being the energy sucker or emotional vampire. It's easy to accuse others and see faults outside of ourselves, but when we sit and reflect with honesty, we find we are guilty of the same accusations.

Who are these people? They are those who dump their shit on you. They suck the life out of you and drain your energy. Dealing with them affects other areas of your life and dims your light. It could be a family member you feel obligated to take shit from or a boss you don't dare tell to get lost.

Low self-esteem is the root cause for one to become an energy sucker or emotional vampire. And there are two types:

1. A person who is going through a crisis and dumping it on you

2. A narcissist who gets a kick out of manipulating and controlling you

Great! Now that we can identify them as buggers in our lives, the question is how to deal with them.

· Set a time limit for interacting with them. Use any excuse to explain that you can't give them all the time in the world, but keep it brief.

· Don't undermine their feelings by saying they are invalid because they already think the world is out to get them. Say, "I hear you," "I feel your pain," "That must be frustrating," or simply, "Mm-hmm, yes, true."

· Neutralize their effect on you. Say, "I care about you, but I'm in a good mood right now, so we can't sit and mope around all day."

· Remember that you may inspire change in them if you speak up and be honest about what is going on and how it makes you feel.

· Get support from positive people you have in your life, and bring more of these types of people into your life.

Who are the positive people you want to surround yourself with?

· They make an effort.

· They are truly happy for you.

· They are upbeat and focus on the positive.

· They are up for anything.

· They have that unmistakable authenticity about them.

Now, contemplate this question: What will you do differently going forward in your interactions with others?

Angry? Who, Me? Never!

All the misery on the planet arises due to a personalized sense of "me" or "us." That covers up the essence of who you are. When you are unaware of that inner essence, in the end, you always create misery. It's as simple as that. When you don't know who you are, you create a mind-made self as a substitute for your beautiful divine being and cling to that fearful and needy self.

—Eckhart Tolle

A wrench thrown into the way we communicate in relationships is anger. When it takes over, we communicate less and less and eventually turn into a ticking bomb. Everyone wants to avoid us at that point, but the poor person you're angry with gets the worst of it. Anger gets in the way of love. But beneath all anger is fear. Here's that *F* word again. I know we dealt with it earlier, but hear me out, please.

Anger is just the aggressive expression of fear. And fear is the nonaggressive expression of anger.

When fear turns into anger, there's little time to react, so we react unintelligently and without awareness. Even when our anger is silent, it's cruel. We become indifferent to others. We sometimes don't even recognize ourselves when we're angry because we turn into horrible people. It's all about us. We're afraid of what will happen to us. We become angry with the very people we care for and love. We're unaware, and therefore, the words that come out are hurtful and poisonous. Then we fall into the guilt trap. Then we apologize. If the apology doesn't work, we again get caught up in anger, a vicious cycle. Our thoughts become even more negatively exaggerated, and we forget all the beautiful things that once existed about the person or the situation.

We become obsessed with anger. Obsessed with the sense of control it gives us. It becomes a habit, a way of coping with issues. A red flag we wave at anyone challenging us—"I'm angry; stay away. I can be destructive or explode in your face" is the message or vibe we're giving off. You become the director, writer, and producer of the dramatic saga that you're about to play out.

If you're smiling and thinking, *Oh, that's so much like me,* you're a person at war with yourself all the time. And if you're at war with yourself, how can you build loving relationships? How can you attract or keep your ideal partner?

One way to look at it is to see anger as your friend. It's not necessarily a nice friend, but it most certainly is a loyal one because it will let you know every single time your values have been trespassed. It will call you to act; it makes you know it's time to take action. Little is taught about how to use our anger energy to clarify our values and strengthen our character, our self-esteem, and our relationships. So the anger itself isn't the solution but the trigger to take the actions necessary to reach a solution, deal with fears, and make things better.

We all have a right to allow ourselves to feel any emotion. But when it comes to anger, we owe it to ourselves to ask, "What is it I'm angry about?" In her book *The Dance of Anger: A Woman's Guide to Changing the Patterns of Intimate Relationships*, Harriet Lerner, PhD, explains that it may seem we have one of two options. One is to vent it all out, explode externally, and exercise our right to full expression, wreaking havoc with our relationships through ineffective fighting and complaining, and then risk being called neurotic and irrational, leaving the real issue underneath all that anger unaddressed. The other is to be the "nice guy" and suppress it, avoiding anger at any cost and letting it fester inside till the point at which we explode internally, thinking we are silent but also wreaking havoc with everyone around us by blocking them out, distancing ourselves from them, or being passive-aggressive. People who suppress anger mask it with feelings of guilt, unworthiness, and self-doubt. The right to express is suppressed, and the voice is muted.

Victims of both these options suffer deeply. It doesn't have to be that way. We get little education in schools or at home on how to effectively deal with anger. We learn only through the examples and patterns we experience or witness, and we avoid it, fear it, do not talk about it, or deny it.

Issues we don't address with our family from childhood are replicated in our future relationships. In *Getting the Love You Want: A Guide for Couples*, Harville Hendrix, PhD, explains how we're attracted to a mate who possesses the same basic qualities as our parents because we subconsciously seek relationships with those who will exorcise our childhood pain. Unfortunately, it doesn't always work, and the anger is compounded as we fall into a destructive pattern in our relationships.

Internally, we struggle because of anger between wanting to have a relationship by doing or being what pleases our partner and wanting to have our own identity by doing or being what pleases us. One of the major triggers of anger is when we want to have control. We want to control not only our decisions, actions, choices, likes, and dislikes, but also other people's decisions, actions, choices, likes, and dislikes! The problem is that it's impossible to achieve that kind of control. It isn't our job to control how anyone reacts to anything. Let them sit with their own feelings, and you sit with yours. Dealing with our own emotions is a load of its own; why take on someone else's emotional load, too?

Sometimes we have very good intentions behind why we want to control. It can be because we think we know better, and we want to rescue or help another person. What I'm about to say is very important. (Time to bust out your highlighter again.) You don't need to rescue, to react, or to fix someone else without their explicit permission. It isn't your responsibility. We can barely rescue ourselves, and look at how well that's going for us, so trying to do so for a whole other person is nuts. They have to acknowledge they need help before anything else and then allow you to help. And if what we do doesn't help, we should let it be.

When we help, we should let go of the outcome. Instead, we double up on our unsuccessful attempts and get even angrier in the process, helping nobody at the end of the day. This isn't compassion. This is very different from the sense of community and connectedness we have when we care for one another and want to help others. This is the result of overinvesting in someone else uninvited. Feeling stressed and angry over it won't serve anyone.

I've been burned a few times this way. Being a life coach, I naturally feel helpless if I don't try to help. But when that help is uninvited, it has the opposite effect on the person, the relationship, and me. On the other hand, we also sometimes feel others are trying to control us, hindering us from doing what we want or trying to change us. Thus, we fall into the angry trap of blaming, complaining, making excuses, and absolving ourselves from the responsibility of making the changes we want or living the life we love. As always, the key is to be clear in our communication—something that's extremely difficult to do when we're angry.

Here's an easy template to use to communicate your exact feeling or emotion that's triggered by someone else's actions without having to attack them or become defensive. Say, "When you [insert action here], it makes me feel [insert emotion here]." For example, "When you arrive late to our appointment, it makes me feel disrespected."

Even if you have to sound like a broken record, keep repeating this till the message is communicated and understood. It's important to keep the description of what the person did as neutral as possible; just state the fact instead of offering a long-winded description about it. You're entitled to your emotions, and this format opens communication channels for a give-and-take to resolve the issue.

There's tons of advice on anger management. What is most important is to learn how to deal with anger in the long run, not just in angry moments. Beneath anger are unresolved past issues. Use your anger as a tool to grow so you'll have better skills in dealing with people and begin to have more fulfilling relationships in the future. Let anger be your motivator to get yourself out of old habits and patterns that don't serve you in being fully yourself. Stay tuned into when anger arises in you, and make it an opportunity to learn more about you and your triggers. Sit with your anger and learn from it. What is it telling you? Which of your values or beliefs is being trespassed, causing the anger? Listen. Makes notes. Learn. Grow.

Your quality of life is equal to the quality of your emotions. Some people can't handle their emotions and escape them by any means possible. We are much more than our emotions. We must be observers of them, not slaves to them.

The older you get, the more you'll realize that friends come and go. The true ones who really have your back will stick around for life, and that's all you need. They're the ones who'll also help you deal with your emotions instead of turning them against you as different ones—including anger—arise.

I dream of a day when the love in each and every one of us is unleashed and magnified to fill our own souls, our lives, the people around us, and our world. I dream of a day when no girl or boy has to be left feeling unloved and grow up trying to compensate for it. I dream of a day when every woman, young or old, won't need a man to justify her significance but instead finds it through her own expression of love for herself and the world.

Exercise

Fill in the blank:

- There would be more love in the world if only people would _____.

- There would be more love in the world if only I would _____.

See how the second phrase brings the responsibility right into my lap? Whereas the first phrase is me waiting for other people to fix the problems of the world. It's up to me. I have to own it. I have to do my part. And so do you.

Chapter 11

Your Mind Wants to Create

Imagination is everything. It is the preview of life's coming attractions.

—Albert Einstein

THE mind wants to create. It wants to put something out there in the world. We are all creators. We all have the urge to create something that's uniquely us. Yet the mind also is the biggest hurdle to jump; it's the one thing that keeps telling you, "No, you can't."

If I told you that I'm a firewalker, as in I walk barefoot on burning coal, what would you say? What's the first thing you'd want to ask me about it? Do I burn my feet? If I told you I swam with nurse sharks in Belize, what would you say? The mind says, "No way; it's impossible," until you do it, and just like that, it's no longer impossible. Like when I climbed to the top of a pole in Fiji that was sixty feet high and jumped off. There was no safety net, only a harness, and my mind said, "No way. I'm not doing that. It's impossible." Then I did it.

The mind tells us we're crazy to do things that are out of our comfort zone, but that's exactly where we want to be. Outside our comfort zone is where all the excitement happens. Risk is there, and when there is risk, life is even more exciting. It needs to be just difficult enough to be called a challenge, yet just easy enough to be doable and fun so that you want to do it.

Exercise

This is a quick exercise to show you how you can go beyond what your mind tells you that you can and can't do.

1. Stand up.

2. Stretch your right arm in front of you and look at your fingertips. Then rotate clockwise at the waist to the farthest point you can reach without moving your firmly grounded feet. Go to the very maximum point you can rotate to, where your mind tells you, "I can't go any farther," and mark that spot with something on the wall or a piece of furniture.

3. Release and go back to your starting position without moving from your spot.

4. Close your eyes, and without moving your body, simply visualize yourself putting your arm in front of you just as you did before. Then visualize yourself rotating all the way to the maximum point that you marked on the wall.

5. Visualize that you go even farther than the original point.

6. Open your eyes, and do the exact same exercise that you just visualized.

If you followed the instructions exactly, you most definitely went farther the second time. Ladies and gentlemen, this is the power of visualization. Never, ever believe all the thoughts that come into your mind. Your mind will stop you from going past your comfort zone every chance it has. And it's your mind that also will take you beyond your wildest dreams.

You Reap What You Sow

All our dreams can come true—if we have the courage to pursue them.

—Walt Disney

I want you to think of your mind as a garden. We're all given the same pack of seeds. We all have the seed of anger, the seed of compassion, the seed of love. We need to be conscious of which seeds we consistently choose to plant, nurture, and grow. We need to be mindful of the soil that needs to be tilled regularly so that it doesn't become arid and infertile.

What do you plant in that garden? You reap what you sow. Your mind is the biggest and most important garden.

Your thoughts become emotions, and your emotions turn into and trigger action.

We have the ability to increase our happiness according to how well we manage our mind and the thoughts, expectations, and beliefs it creates. The mind constantly tries to match expectations with actual experiences and is often disappointed because the world will never match the conceptual model the mind has made up.

Let me elaborate. I created a vision board in 2013 that was all about health and fitness. On that board, I had two different pictures of women holding surfboards. My mind said, "No way." My mind decided that the image didn't match the reality of my chronic back pain and inflexibility. But I became more mindful of my health and exercised a lot more because I had placed the board in my room where it was the first thing I looked at when I woke up and the last thing I looked at before I slept. Two years later, I found myself in Sri Lanka at a surfing school, and within a week, I was surfing a green wave. Me! Surfing!

Here's another true story. In July 2016, I was in Spain at a "Life Mastery" course with Tony Robbins. In one of the exercises, we had to push ourselves beyond our comfort zones, and it was then and there that I set an intention and wrote it down. I put in writing that I'd do the yoga-teacher training course. And in that moment, I was already thinking, *Yeah, right!*

Let me give you a clearer picture of why my mind thought it was a far-fetched goal. As a kid, my dear family had a nickname for me: Teakwood. I was the most inflexible kid as far as the eye could see. Short hamstrings, tight hips, chronic back pain. You name it; I have it. I started yoga some twenty years ago, on and off. I went to many yoga retreats in exotic locations and always tried to challenge myself to go thirty days of practicing daily so I could gain more flexibility and strength. Never happened.

Exactly one year after setting the intention, I found myself at a yoga-teacher training course in Thailand. That's a loaded program from 7:00 a.m. to 7:00 p.m. for a month. I'm still in disbelief. But one of the things I also wrote down many years ago is that I wanted my body to constantly amaze me with what it can do. Writing things down is intergalactically important. Set that intention on paper in black and white. Then it's real.

Your thoughts become your reality. We need to be careful what we plant in our garden, who we allow into it, and how we maintain it. Your mind is like a five-year-old child, susceptible to anything she hears. Would you let someone tamper with your kid's mind and tell her about horrid world news? Would you expose her to negative shit in newspapers and on the internet?

If you had a beautiful home full of the finest furniture, curtains, and area rugs all in white, would you let just anyone waltz through it with muddy boots? Of course not. So why, then, would you let the media and politicians pollute your mind with their toxins? We live like walking, talking zombies, unaware and unconscious for the most part. We allow negative, debilitating, and disempowering thoughts to roam around our minds like unwelcome guests walking with muddy shoes around our house. False ideas, false concepts, and false beliefs stop us from living our passions and fully expressing our true selves. We're so out of touch with our center—our core—and don't even realize how trapped we are in a prison of our own making. If others try to wake us up, we fight them. We accuse them of not knowing what they're talking about. We become blinded by our habits.

We need to empty the mind of the junk of doing so we can have room to receive and appreciate the gift of mindfully being. This way, we have more room to scoop big buckets of the infinite ocean of love, spice, and everything nice rather than just cupfuls. If your mind is full of "I know," there's no room for you to learn and grow.

We live in a time of stress, anxiety, and being overwhelmed. We're constantly rushing, racing, wanting to multitask and do more and more. And to stay trapped in our comfort zone, we believe crippling thoughts like *there's not enough time.* Our minds are full of thoughts and beliefs and inner chatter. In her book *Happy for No Reason: 7 Steps to Being Happy from the Inside Out*, Marci Shimoff says that according to scientists, we have about sixty thousand thoughts per day; 95 percent of those thoughts are recycled from our past, and 80 percent of them are negative. Do the math. That's one negative thought per minute of our waking time. And just so you know, our subconscious mind doesn't really stop working when we're asleep. Dr. Daniel Amen, a world-renowned psychiatrist and brain-imaging specialist, discovered automatic negative thoughts—or ANTS. These ANTS impact your mood, your decision-making, your actions, your health, and your relationships. But just as you can't believe everything you see on the news or you read on the internet or you hear through gossip, you can't believe or subscribe to or engage with every thought you have. We can't possibly believe every one of those thoughts. You aren't what you think; you're what you believe.

Negativity is like Velcro, and positivity slides off like Teflon. Fixation on delusions and obsessions is your worst enemy. It clouds your inner peace so you can't see clearly. It's the enemy of your self-growth and inner happiness. Once you separate yourself from your thoughts and become an observer of them, you've won your lottery ticket to freedom from suffering.

Compare your entire being to a battery. There are two ends. One is positive, the other negative. One is an expanding potential of what we can create and do with our lives, and the other is contracting. And you are the boss of it all. You get to choose which direction you go. You have the capacity, power, and freedom to go either way.

Who can do this? Everyone. When should you do this? Now. How can you do it? We are our own holistic nutritionist. We choose our own cure for a better, more positive mix of thoughts to fill our minds with a prescription of decisions coming from the center of our core essence, where everything is pure and simple. We all have it, yet we ignore it. We don't seek it, nurture it, or tap into its infinite energy.

We're taught to be good boys and girls from an early age. We're loved for what we do, not for who we are. So we grow up with a mentality that pushes us to achieve, to do more and better all the time. We turn into anal, obsessive-compulsive freaks. We take life too seriously, and if someone dares to tell us to chill, we're offended.

Up until very recently, I was so guilty of that. I was competing with my own shadow and wouldn't give myself a break. When I first started Be You International, I hardly took a weekend off. I was always tapped into my masculine energy, wanting to be perfect, efficient, able to do more in less time. I forgot I was a woman first and foremost. I got stressed beyond words and lost all interest in maintaining a proper social life. Luckily, I grew up. I remembered there's a feminine side to me that I need to nurture just as much. Now I'm more about being than about doing, and somehow, I'm achieving more, and it's happening effortlessly.

One thing is essential for all this to happen: the desire to change. We need to choose to be comfortable with being uncomfortable outside our comfort zone. We must have the willingness to be open, allow ourselves to be vulnerable, be hungry for a more mindful life. We aren't afraid of our shadow; it's our light that terrifies us. How will we ever shine with the magnificence of being ourselves, of being who we really are, if we're afraid of how brightly that light will shine?

A sane mind never suffers; it only grows. Learn to look forward to mistakes because through them, your mind grows even more. Be grateful for the friction in your life and relationships, for they polish you into a stronger being. And that's how you evolve. In one experiment, two German psychologists, Sascha Topolinski and Fritz Strack, found that mood has a powerful effect on performance. Just by asking the participants to think of a pleasant memory or a happy thought, their accuracy in problem solving increased by 100 percent. The participants who were asked to think of unpleasant or unhappy thoughts were unable to solve the problem, and their guesses were no better than random. When we're in a bad mood, our mind doesn't function well, and we're not tapped into our intuition.

Words: They Can Build You Up or Break You Down

Success, like happiness, cannot be pursued. It must ensue. And it only does so as the unintended side effect of one's personal dedication to a cause greater than oneself.

—Viktor E. Frankl

You have to be mindful of the dictionary you create from childhood—the dictionary that tells you what words and events and situations mean. I said it before, and I will say it again: nothing has meaning but the meaning you give it. And you give meaning to things from your own perspective. A perspective you don't question but refer to blindly.

Sometimes your vision conflicts with your inner intuition. Sometimes you have to close your eyes and see with your third eye—the eye of your inner wisdom—where you'll find absolute truth. After all, we've all experienced being wrong and proving others wrong. Being stubborn is a dangerous thing. Being honest with yourself and being vulnerable can end the illusion of being manipulated in any way. When you are genuinely humble, there's no place for criticism or negativity to stick.

One of the four agreements that Don Miguel Ruiz talks about in his book *The Four Agreements: A Practical Guide to Personal Freedom (A Toltec Wisdom Book)* is to be impeccable with your words. Here's what I learned from it. Words can build you up, and they can break you down. Words have their own energy. And some words can suck the energy right out of you. They have that lingering aftereffect, but only because we hold on to them so tightly. These words turn into stories, and the stories make us feel an emotion or an ocean of emotions! Remember, our minds want to create. Leave your mind idle, and it will create just about any story.

Words can hurt. Forget about sticks and stones—words once uttered set a chain reaction in motion that's sometimes irreversible. Like a chipped vase, even if it's only a fine crack, you always know it's there. Words can be potent and poisonous. Some can leave you with a hollow feeling in your stomach. Painful ones can linger for years or even a lifetime, reminding you of the pain at every opportunity.

Luckily for us, words can heal, too. Words can take you on a journey to cloud nine and back. Words can make you say yes to a lifetime commitment. Words can bring you joy and love that nothing can describe! If words of affirmation are your love language, you know exactly what I'm talking about.

In one workshop I attended about relationships, I learned that women use five thousand to seven thousand words on average per day while men use only two thousand to three thousand. And that's just spoken words. We're not even counting self-talk. That's a lot of words, and what are you doing with them? Open your heart before you open your mouth. With love, you learn to create. You use your words to spread love and communicate clarity and build constructive lives.

Without love, you learn to destroy. You use your words to spread poison and hatred, communicate lies, pass on gossip, make false assumptions, and ruin your life. Assumptions are made because we are afraid to ask. We are so isolated or feel that way, and we just want to defend our ego.

Speak the truth. Period. Forget about white lies and black lies. Even the CIA has its own system of classification of lies and a color code. So, you have white, gray, and black propaganda. Can you believe that? Even withholding the truth is a lie if you want to get technical. And it's not just what you say but how you say it that could be the lie. Isn't it much easier to speak the truth? Your truth. Life is much simpler that way. Trust me on that one.

Before you utter another word for the rest of your life, ask yourself four questions.

1. Is what I'm about to say true?

2. Is it necessary?

3. Is it kind?

4. Does it come from a place of love?

This is powerful inner reflection, especially with heated conversations and problematic relationships where you feel you are being criticized or you need to justify yourself. Justifications can be stressful. Are yours an attempt to manipulate? Are you being unnecessarily defensive?

Bring more awareness to how often you use words like *because* or *but* as you speak. Words like *but* separate and often negate anything you said right before it. Instead, use the word *and*, which joins. Each time you notice you're justifying, defending, apologizing, or using the words *because, or*, and *but*, stop speaking immediately. Notice how it feels to interrupt yourself. Journal your thoughts, and you'll see how you start to communicate what you want to say more efficiently.

What kills the spark and joy of any relationship is criticism. It comes from fear. Criticism is nothing more or less than an ineffective way of pleading for love. Criticize and your partner will disengage. Try to control and your partner will also disengage. The louder the criticism, the deeper the emotional need. When we understand what criticism is really about, we find that it's one of the most powerful tools for self-realization and growth. If you listen carefully, it will also provide clues to the person's love language. Mark Manson, the author of *The Subtle Art of Not Giving a F*ck: A Counterintuitive Approach to Living a Good Life*, lays it out beautifully when he says that in relationships, it has to be a clear "fuck yes" or a clear "fuck no" about *something*; otherwise, you're just wasting your time[8].

With awareness, proper communication, and genuine love, even a negative emotion like jealousy can enrich relationships, rekindle passion, renew commitment, and amplify the attention two people pay to each other. I invite you to make a list of the people you need to make amends with. Think of it as the list to free yourself from all negativity.

Nobody on the earth is better than Byron Katie and her amazing work at facilitating the process of freeing yourself from the crap you hold on to forever. Making amends is about clearing up your life. Here's how she explains it in her "School for the Work," an amazing nine-day experience[9] that I believe is a must for just about anyone.

- Find the people, dead or alive, you need to make amends with, and start an amends list. Include yourself.

- Remember the times when you hurt someone. You could ask yourself, "Who did I ignore to punish them? Who else do I criticize in my mind or in my life?" It's best to make amends face-to-face when possible; otherwise, the phone, a letter, or email will do. As you talk with them, notice if you move mentally into their business (meaning you are interfering in what they did or said). Notice how it feels inside to be in someone else's business, judging them again. If you see yourself doing that, *stop*. Move back into your own business and start again.

- When making amends with yourself, be real. Take each point in, and feel and experience it deeply. Ask yourself, "Was I doing the best I could with all the information I had at that particular time?"

Exercise

Think of someone you criticize often or someone you actually hate. This is one fun exercise when you really need to stretch your mind. I had a blast doing this exercise on Donald Trump!

Now write down three things you hate about this person that he/she needs to change. Then ask yourself, "How do I do each of those things I listed? Where? With whom? When?" Take your time with this, and think of even the smallest example of when you were guilty of what you hate about that person. Learn from this new awareness. We are all mirrors for one another to learn and grow. We can all turn into Adolf Hitlers or Mother Teresas.

When someone says you're wrong, unkind, unclear, and uncaring, feel it. Settle into it before you react. Experience it before opening your mouth to respond. Ask yourself, "Is it true? Could they be right?" Wait for the answer. You have to be totally mindful and have elasticity in your mind; then you can stretch yourself beyond your restricting belief system, and new answers will come from within. Nothing is more dangerous than a stubborn mind that isn't open to a different way of seeing things. I like how you say *a closed mind* in Spanish, *una cabeza cerrado*. Don't have one of those minds. Please, don't be that person!

If the criticism you received is causing you stress or pain, that's a sign that you believe the criticism is true, and you haven't dealt with it or gone deeply enough yet. If you want to end the war in your own life and mind, you may decide to gently go deeper as you inquire and discover the truth of the criticism within yourself. When you have an issue, own it. It's yours, all yours to deal with. This is where all wars end.

No matter what anyone says to you or about you, if you experience stress, you're the one who is suffering from your hidden secret—the secret you hide even from yourself in the moment—and the mind will do its job, which is to attack. Your own mind's attack is the cause of stress. Stress is the signal that it's time to ask, time to inquire; it's an opportunity for you to know the truth. Stress is always an opportunity to experience forgiveness for the people you judge and for those who judge you so you can end the stress within you. Forgiveness can't be found anywhere else.

Be mindful of your words and the vocabulary you regularly use. Which of the following statements is something you commonly say or believe in?

"People are out to get me."

"People are so helpful."

"It's a cruel world."

"It's a beautiful world."

"Karma is a bitch."

"Karma is what you make it."

Each of these statements or beliefs will create different experiences that you manifest through the type of vocabulary and choice of words you use frequently.

> *I slept and dreamed that life was joy. I awoke and saw that life was service. I acted, and behold, service was joy.*
>
> —Rabindranath Tagore

Ever since that dream I had in Ancaster that I told you about earlier, I knew what it was that I was here to do. How I was going to do that was a totally different story! I didn't have a clue. All I knew was that I was at the furthest point from that dream. I was not in the right career, and I did not have any background in teaching or education. The closest I ever got to teaching was coaching my baby sister, who is twenty years younger.

So how did my mind process all this? It gave me every reason to disregard the whole thing. Sadly, that's what I did at that time in my life. I felt stuck where I was and completely unsupported and gave up before I had even started. But the dream and the thoughts around it lived on! It was like a little voice that spoke out every so often. A little shy voice among a million other voices shutting it up by saying things like "Focus on work. Make money. Lose weight. Save the marriage. Work your to-do list for the day." Sound familiar? I'm sure you have the same things going on that silence the one voice you really want to hear!

The mind just wants to get busy, and if we don't give it something constructive to do, it will get busy on the mundane. More specifically, as research shows, it will go back to thinking about past relationships.

Signs showed up that pointed me back to my life's purpose. They were in the form of a dream or a friend wanting to connect me with someone who could potentially help me with my mission. It just felt like things were falling into place effortlessly … and I took it all as a sign that I was heading in the right direction. I would think of what small step I could take in that direction and take it. Tiny steps were what I made, almost like trying not to be seen taking them because of fear or because I knew I had "more important" things to do, or just because I didn't believe I could do much about it.

With time, I managed to work my way through the immediate two major challenges in the way of making that dream come true. I got out of the marriage, and I quit my real estate career. Neither was an easy task, especially with the depression, the breakdown, and the burnout that followed. It was in that last burned-out timeout from life that the doors started opening. The answer to how I would realize my dream started to form. I knew where I was heading, and that was the most important thing. It was all I needed to know at that moment. No more lies and excuses.

We practice the doing, doing, and doing, but we also need to practice the stopping. Stop thinking, stop planning, stop running, stop judging, stop everything, and enjoy just being. Whenever I'm stressed, I say this to myself: "I have nothing to do, and I have nowhere to go in this moment. It gives me peace because it allows me to stop and breathe and notice." To notice is a very important thing. Have I mentioned that already? If we don't practice noticing, we will miss out on this moment. We will miss out on so many beautiful things happening around us. Notice … and all you need to do to notice is to slow down.

We say life is a journey, and we are eager to get to the destination. In the grand scheme of things, the final destination is death. So why hurry? Go in the direction of life, and that is this moment. It is so easy to get there. All you have to do is breathe in and smile, breathe out and smile.

In his book *The Power of Now: A Guide to Spiritual Enlightenment*, Eckhart Tolle describes the mind as a tool. And as with most tools, once a task is completed, you put the tool down. Yet we don't. Our minds want to think all the time, and we can't stop; 80–90 percent of our thinking is repetitive and useless, and because of its negative nature, it's also harmful. That's exactly what an addiction is. It's something we can't stop, and it gives us a false sense of pleasure that turns into pain. And as long as you're in that pain, in your mind, you aren't being mindful. Mindfulness is your ticket to freedom, your liberation from pain. Then your mind's main focus becomes removing that pain, which causes even more repetition and harm to your emotional state in that moment.

At the beginning of this book, I mentioned a Vipassana retreat I attended. Just before leaving home to go there, my dad and I had an argument as he decided I should cancel. It's a long story, and the short of it is that without any proper explanation, he wanted me to obey as if I were a fifteen-year-old. I didn't. I decided to stick to my plan, and I went. It was a three- or four-hour drive to Ras Al Khaimah from Abu Dhabi, where I live. During the drive, Dad called me when he realized I had gone after all and said very unkind words. That incident repeated in my head throughout the drive.

When I arrived, we had to surrender all our communication devices. So, I switched the phone off and gave it away. And with that, somehow, I switched off the story with Dad and all that had happened in the last twelve hours or so. I figured I was going to be stuck in meditation with nowhere to go, so I'd worry about that problem when I got back home.

During ten days of silent meditation, I hardly thought about that problem again. What I did think about over and over again, though, was a relationship that had gone bad and ended six months earlier! The madness that's called the brain, eh?

These repetitive and incessant thoughts you carry around have an impact on your body. You hold angry thoughts, your body contracts, and you "feel" anger. Then you start attracting it or attracting reasons to feel even angrier. It almost doesn't matter anymore what your morals are or what values you honor. When your mind is clouded, all that matters and has more power over you is where you put your focus and attention. Then you drift and become unaware of how out of control you are, all the while fully believing you're in control. That's what unawareness is.

Mindfulness allows you to accept the emotion as a stand-alone without being suckered into it and reacting to it. It allows you to watch but not analyze. It allows you to refrain rather than react. That's being emotionally intelligent. That's being in control of your emotions rather than vice versa. Moments of total bliss or joy or peace are experienced only when the mind's stream of thoughts stops or takes a pause.

Mindfulness is the total opposite of multitasking. Once upon a time, I used to take pride in how many things I could juggle at the same time. It fried my brain cells, but that didn't matter because I was ticking things off my list like there was no tomorrow. But research done at Stanford University shows that those who think they are great multitaskers actually suck at it. They just don't notice their mistakes and the errors created along the way or how poorly they perform because they're, well, too busy to notice! Multitasking is just rapidly switching your attention among things. Earl Miller, a neuroscientist at MIT, explains that this increases your margin of errors and actually decreases your productivity. He says the ceaseless onslaught of information has the potential to cripple us as our brains are not equipped to handle the sensory overload of multitasking. You are far better off getting into what psychologist Mihaly Csikszentmihalyi calls "flow." When you are in flow, you are totally mindful and completely immersed in that one task you are doing without any distractions, and therefore, you are automatically way more creative and productive at it.

I left my phone at home the other day. When I noticed, I thought I could make do without it for a day with no issues. Little did I know how wrong I was. I couldn't use the app to pay for my parking when I got to the office. I didn't know the time all day because I don't wear a watch. I couldn't confirm my appointments, which I usually do through WhatsApp. I couldn't take a picture of the beautiful view outside my window—something I often do.

It made me realize a few things. Our phones make us so hyperconnected and wired and prone to multitasking all the time. We're constantly checking our emails, messages, and apps and feel like we're constantly on the go, rushing to get that to-do list done. This activates the fight-or-flight mode in our brains. It's like we're running away from a dinosaur that's out to get us. But we'll never be fast enough. What's more dangerous than being eaten by a dinosaur is being beaten down by our constant worry about time and our to-do lists. So stop telling kids to hurry up in the morning. Stop cramming things into your day and a million appointments into your calendar. Sometimes even going to the spa becomes a chore. That's not how we should live. That's definitely not how I want to. There's more than enough time for everything, and everything will happen in its own time, very much like the gorgeous snow flowers I used to plant in my backyard in Burlington, Ontario, around October. Then I'd forget about them until I was surprised to see them bloom through the heaps of snow in February. A very happy moment.

I invite you to do what I do. Do not multitask at all. Or keep it down to the bare minimum, to be realistic. Focus on activities and tasks that are important but not urgent. Things like planning for the future and building relationships are important, long-term goals. And focusing on them decreases your crisis time and shrinks the problems you believe are urgent because you're focusing on what matters, planning in advance, and thinking ahead. According to Stephen R. Covey, author of *The 7 Habits of Highly Effective People: Powerful Lessons in Personal Change*, this increases your effectiveness[10].

Stress is a signal that you need to question your thoughts. Byron Katie says the world or money or relationships aren't the problem. It's our thinking that's the problem[11]. I love how she lays out the three kinds of business in the world: my business, your business, and God's business.

- Whose business is it if I'm feeling happy or sad? My business.

- Whose business is it if you're feeling happy or sad? Your business.

- Whose business is the weather? God's business.

Here's an anecdote that's really on point[12]. Four merchants were praying in a mosque when they saw the muezzin enter. The first merchant stopped his prayer and asked, "Muezzin! Has the prayer been called for? Or do we have time?"

The second merchant stopped praying and turned to his friend to tell him that his prayer was now void because he had interrupted it by speaking to the muezzin.

In turn, the third merchant said, "Why do you blame him? You should have minded your own prayer. Now yours is void, too."

The fourth merchant loudly said, "Look at them! All three have messed up. Thank God I'm not one of the misguided."

Why is it so hard for us to mind our own business? Much of our stress occurs when we forget to stick to our own business. When I'm telling you how you should dress, what you should do, how to run your life, or imposing any opinion on you, I'm in your business, not mine. When I'm worried about earthquakes, floods, war, or when I will die, I'm in God's business. If I am mentally in your business or in

God's business, who is minding my own business? Notice when you give uninvited advice either out loud or silently. Whose business are you in when you give unsolicited advice?

When you understand the three kinds of businesses well enough to stay in your own business, you're freed to be completely present in your own life. You're also freed from any victimhood tendencies like complaining, blaming, and feeling shame. You're freed from being the guest of honor at your own pity party. All this is a major threat to your happiness.

Put a jar aside and call it a pity-party fund. For a week, add a dollar for every time you complain, blame, make an excuse, or indulge in self-pity, self-hate, or cruelty. See how fast it fills up.

Touching again on what we've covered in the section on relationships, victimhood is thinking that the past is stronger than the present. It's believing that what happened to you is responsible for who you are now, your pain now, and your inability to be you.

Victimhood brings pain. Pain comes in two forms: one that you create now—in the present—and one from past memories that you relive, never let go of, and don't allow to dissolve. That happens because we have habit centers that keep us in a loop of suffering. And the source of the pain is nonacceptance—resistance to what is, as is. We want to analyze instead of just experience. We hang on tight instead of letting things flow through us. Where there is anger, there is always pain. And pain always surfaces when you are outside of this present moment, when you are reliving the past, where emotions like depression, guilt, regret, resentment, grief, sadness, bitterness, and unforgiveness reign, or living in the future, where emotions like anxiousness, uneasiness, tension, stress, worry, and all forms of fear reign.

Anything you experience or feel happens in the now and cannot exist outside the now. There is no time. Time is not precious. This moment is. It is everything there is. To be free of all negative states is to be present. Consciousness and mindfulness are freedom from all negativity. It's like darkness that can never exist in the presence of light. Daily meditation creates new habits and new ways of witnessing the world around us with detachment from all the headache-inducing nitty-gritty. It's the difference between having a monkey mind, where the reception is bad and you're getting only weak signals, versus a clear mind, where reception is superb. Remember that scary nightmares and beautiful dreams are all fabricated in the mind.

Chapter 12

Your Body Wants to Grow Healthy

*We excel at making a living but often fail at making
a life. We celebrate our prosperity but yearn for purpose. We cherish our freedoms but long for connection. In an age of plenty, we feel spiritual hunger.*

—David G. Myers

OUR body wants to grow healthy. It's truly a miracle to
be alive—a miracle we take for granted. Everything
that happens to us and to our bodies is so we die on time.
Nobody is checking out any sooner or later than the sched-
uled time! Your body is like a house. Sooner or later, it gets
old.

You have a set of eyes that instantly make over ten million different color distinctions. Your nose can distinguish
over ten thousand distinct smells. Your heart beats over one
hundred thousand times a day, pumping over six thousand
quarts of blood. You use seventy-two muscles in perfect co-
ordination to enable speech. You have two hundred and six
bones and around seven hundred muscles that give you freedom to move and the power to push and pull and do crazy

things with your body. All these miracles are run by a body made up of almost 98 percent water and a brain. Your brain is in charge of all your body's systems and is constantly monitoring everything without you even thinking about it. It's a powerhouse like no other. Its power is greater than the fastest, most powerful computer on Earth.

Whether or not you remember to breathe, your lungs keep breathing. You inhale and exhale seven hundred and twenty times an hour; that's more than seventeen thousand times a day. Your heart keeps beating, your stomach keeps digesting, and your lymphatic system keeps cleaning up your body. All this happens without your permission or advice or any instructions.

While we're on this journey called life, taking our chosen road trips, we need to maintain the vehicle that takes us from the cradle to the grave. What's the point of being the happiest person on the planet if you're suffering because you aren't exercising or honoring that body and taking care of that brain? The body is always in the present, here and now. But the mind, not as much, as we've already seen, and therefore, we have anxiety.

By the way, your physical body doesn't need as much rest as your mind needs stimulation. When your mind is occupied with something you are excited about, you can go with a few hours of sleep and still jump out of bed with so much energy and vigor. When your mind is weighed down with worry and stress that directly affects your body, you wake up sluggish, even if you had a full night's worth of good quality sleep.

With all this incredible, miraculous power within you, you can accomplish any goal you desire. But without maintenance, all your life goals will just remain dreams. And this powerhouse becomes your primary pain in the ass! Isn't it time to take charge and appreciate this body of yours?

Once upon a Time in Tepoztlán, Mexico

To laugh often and much; to win the respect of intelligent people and the affection of children; to earn the appreciation of honest critics and endure the betrayal of false friends; to appreciate beauty, to find the best in others; to leave the world a bit better, whether by a healthy child, a garden patch, or a redeemed social condition; to know even one life has breathed easier because you have lived. This is to have succeeded.

—Bessie A. Stanley

"See the mountain ahead?" Marco, my friend, asks.

"Yes, I do," I say.

"Look at the very top, just below that cloud on the left. Do you see that temple?" He guides me to look way up toward the cloud as I squint, searching for what he wants me to see. Then I find it.

"Yes, I see it," I say.

"Well, we're gonna hike up to that temple," he says.

"Sure, we will," I reply sarcastically, thinking he's just pulling my leg. Turns out, he wasn't!

Up we go, a group of five. Up we go for almost two hours! I was the youngest of the lot, at thirty-five, and definitely the most unfit. I was huffing and puffing all the way like nobody's business. Had to take a few dozen breaks to catch my breath and to drink some water and to kick myself for accepting the invitation to go on this hike.

To give you some background information about my fitness level at that stage in my life, my idea of climbing was limited to climbing onto my sofa with a bowl of popcorn to watch a movie. My idea of a marathon was watching several *CSI* or *Sex in the City* episodes in a row. My workload was too much. I didn't have the time to go to the gym or even look at myself in the mirror. I had just gone through a divorce. My mind wasn't in the right place. Exercise was the last of my priorities. I was basically letting myself go health-wise.

So, this hike was my wake-up call. How could the others —one who was fifty years old—race past me like they were taking a stroll in the park and not this treacherous hike that felt like going up to the sun? Marco repeatedly whizzed by. He came back for me, then went back up to join the fast group, then returned to me—just imagine how healthy he was. In my mind, I was only contrasting that with my condition. Every time he came by, he would say, "Let it go. With every step, shed it, and you will feel lighter."

I didn't understand him. I didn't get it at the time. I was just hoping I was closer to the end of this torture session. Feeling sorry for myself, I sat down by some boulder and cried. I cried because I wanted out. I cried because of the shame I'd feel if I were to go back. I cried because I looked ahead and saw the crack between the two mountains that was even higher in altitude and how far I still had to go. I had no idea how much longer the hike was going to take. I couldn't see the end. I cried most of all because I was feeling sorry for myself. I was thinking of how pathetic I was. That break took the longest.

"Let it go. Let it go. Let it all go." Those words kept ringing in my head. I decided to continue the hike. My friends had to be at the top by now, at that temple drinking mojitos and singing "Kumbaya." I had to join them. I decided to push myself and let go with every step. Let go of my past. Let go of the failed marriage. Let go of long hours of work. Let go of an unrewarding life. Let go of ignoring my body. Let go of an unfit life. Let go of all the negativity and the tears. Let go of what other people think or say. Let it all go.

I was welcomed at the top with a cheering band. I finally got to the friggin' temple. We stayed there for a while. No mojitos, but they did have a refreshing lemonade-like beverage that I gulped down in two seconds. Marco led us through an awesome sound meditation with our voices echoing beautifully against the rocks. In that moment, as I was oohing, eeing, and awwing, I realized that when it gets tough, that's when you need to push through the hardest. And that the pushing can be something as simple as letting go.

One of the first things I did as soon as I was back in Canada was to go to the gym on an almost daily basis, and I cut down on the popcorn and junk food in front of the TV. In fact, I sold the TV altogether.

We come from Earth, and back to Earth we go. A farmer invests so much time and effort into his piece of land. Each season has its own part of the process that it needs to achieve during that season. It cannot be slowed down or sped up. It will all come out accordingly in its right time during the harvest, and you reap what you sow.

The condition of your body is just like that farm. What you have been doing with it in your twenties, you will experience in your thirties. What you do in your thirties, you will feel in your forties, etcetera. Some people are well into their sixties, seventies, or even eighties, and they look younger and, more importantly, feel younger. Some people are in their twenties but look and feel as if they have the burden of decades already taking their toll on them.

I turned forty a few years ago, and I have never felt younger physically. All thanks go to the transformative experience I had at Tony Robbins's "Unleash the Power Within" event. Right after that event, I got myself registered for a ten-kilometer relay race in Abu Dhabi. I had to run 2.5 kilometers, which I'd never done before. I trained as best I could (which was pretty minimal, now that I think back on it), and I gave it all I had on the day of the event. A few months later, I did my first full ten-kilometer run, and I did it again the next year. The year after, I participated in the Desert Warrior Challenge in Dubai—ten kilometers with obstacles—and I was the only woman on my team to surpass all the obstacles. It was amazing.

The body won't go where the mind won't go first. Remember the exercise from the previous section where you rotated your body, and the difference before and after visualization? If the mind can imagine it, the body will follow. That's why Olympic athletes visualize themselves going through the motions of the sport they're about to play. A skier, for example, will go through every little detail while still standing at that start line at the top of the hill. That's how they outperform themselves.

The Greatest Game Ever Played is a biographical movie about amateur-turned-golf-champion Francis Ouimet. The way the movie shows us how he focuses on his swing and where the ball will go is amazing. He totally zones out of everything else. There are no people or noise or anything at all but him, the club in his hand, the ball, and the field ahead. And it really is an enjoyable way to learn about the power of focus and visualization.

Taking care of your body has two parts: the active part and the passive part. Movement and stillness. The doing and the being. Pick something you love to do, and make it your excuse to exercise. Sometimes it needs to be something exciting or challenging so that you have a strong motivation to get up and do it. I'm far too lazy and uninterested to go to the gym. It's such a boring thing to me. So instead, I go on yoga retreats or walk the desert from Al Ain to Abu Dhabi with the Women Heritage Walk in the UAE or learn to surf in Sri Lanka. All these activities require that I be fit, so when something exciting like that is on my calendar, I'm motivated like there's no tomorrow to go for a spinning class or a TRX class and to be religious about planking and doing some abdominal workout every morning. Find yours. Get active. And whatever you do, don't let "perfect" be the enemy of "good." No matter how little you do, it's better than doing nothing at all.

At the time of writing this book, I've just returned to climbing. It's been only a month since I've been back at it, and I already feel the energy of excitement about my progress and am doing extra classes on the side to make my core even stronger. It's an excellent sport that teaches modesty about the raw you and perseverance; you've got to get up there one way or another. It also teaches you to visualize your route and to trust your hands and feet, one step up at a time.

I'm also partial to yoga, regular as well as AcroYoga. That's like playtime for adults, and I look forward to those classes every week. Yoga is a unique exercise that can be made as gentle or as intense as you want it to be. You can burn almost one hundred and seventy calories in one hour of hatha yoga and a lot more during power yoga or vinyasa. Asana, which is the practical part of yoga, contributes to a healthy body and mind. The whole purpose of asana, the active part of yoga, is to prepare the body for stillness during meditation. It helps with your flexibility, increases your muscle strength, and reduces back and joint pain. You'll notice you start performing better at other sports activities —most rock climbers and surfers do yoga regularly. It also reduces stress through lowering your cortisol and adrenaline hormone levels. You become more in tune with your body and the messages it gives you. So you will become a more mindful eater and a kinder person to yourself. The best part about it is that you can practice almost anywhere.

Ancient yogis believed that vigorous walking in nature did wonders to restore the body's vibrant state, unlock vitality, rejuvenate itself, relieve fatigue symptoms, and focus the mind. Studies of monks' brains show they have greater activity in the left prefrontal cortex, orderly heart-wave patterns, and more of the neurotransmitters associated with well-being and happiness, namely oxytocin, serotonin, dopamine, and endorphins.

Travel, if you ask me, is another form of exercise. It stretches the mind, specifically. The stretch is not because of the new experiences and flavors and colors and landscapes we get to enjoy, but from the new knowledge we acquire as we see others doing things differently, shattering our rigid minds and our sometimes unrelenting belief systems about what is right and what is wrong. Preparing for a trip is in itself an exercise as you start your research of the destination in advance or prepare your body for the physical challenge of hiking a mountain you want to summit, joining a yoga retreat, or enrolling in a surfing school. Travel, hands down, is my absolute favorite activity.

Here are some of the benefits of exercise in any form you choose:

- reduces stress and depression

- improves digestion

- decreases body fat and helps control weight

- enhances sexual and mental functions

- lowers blood pressure

- improves cholesterol levels

- strengthens your cardiovascular system

- boosts metabolism

- improves sleep

- improves your flexibility and overall strength

Shhh! Time to Sit Still and Meditate

One hour's meditation on the work of the creator is better than seventy years of prayer.

—Prophet Muhammad

The second part of how to take care of your body is through stillness.

Our body is a tool, and if we don't rest that tool, we will suffer consequences. A study by Daniel Kahneman and colleagues, published in *Science* (2004), calculated that for those who are sleep deprived, one extra hour of sleep could do more for their daily happiness than a raise. That same study showed that there is no correlation between extra money earned and one's happiness level. Another study conducted from 2005–2010 by the Centers for Disease Control and Prevention revealed that nine million people in the United States need prescription sleeping aids[13]. Not having enough quality sleep is serious business. Arianna Huffington, the cofounder and editor-in-chief of the *Huffington*

Post, woke up one morning in a pool of her own blood on the floor of her home office. She had been on the phone and checking emails when she literally fell from exhaustion, breaking her cheekbone as her head hit the corner of her desk. After weeks of medical tests, the conclusion was that she was suffering from exhaustion and lack of sleep. That fall was the turning point in her life, as she describes in her book *Thrive*.

Like water, the mind is ever moving, ever changing, never stopping, and never ending, with strings of thought after thought. With meditation, the aim is not to stop this flow but rather to become more selective about which thoughts we want to engage with. You are not your thoughts; you are the creator of those thoughts. The difference is huge, and just as you created one type of thought, you can create another type, a more forgiving and less stressful kind. Freedom from stress is your conscious effort to choose one thought over another. The answers, though—that inner wisdom—are achieved only when we are able to still the mind. It's a lot easier to still the mind when your body is still. You have to freeze water so you can look at the perfection of the snowflake crystals. You cannot see any snowflakes in a river of running water.

One major change that has occurred within our brains through evolution is that we have this section called the prefrontal cortex. This part is what makes our brains bigger than those of all other creatures on Earth. And it is this part that allows us the gift of experiencing things in our minds without having to physically go through the experience.

Take a moment and, with closed eyes, think of someone you love. Feel their presence; recall a beautiful memory with them or a conversation. In this moment, you feel loved and totally absorbed in the feeling of having them present with you. Now, when you open your eyes, the impact that visualization had on you is exactly as if that person were really in the room with you. Your mind can't tell the difference between real and imagined.

Try this again, but this time, imagine you are peeling a lemon, cutting it into quarters, grabbing one, and biting into it. You will have a physical reaction almost equivalent to actually biting into a lemon.

Nurturing this part of the mind through meditation is important. In your mind, you can make anything happen, and then your next step is manifesting it through action.

In standing yoga poses, they always ask that you have a gaze point or a *drishti*; that's a fixed point in the room right in front of you. It's only with that kind of focus on that one point that you can balance yourself into the pose. Looking every which way while trying to balance on one foot getting into any pose would be impossible. That gaze is symbolic of making the mind still. Getting into the pose with grace and balance is symbolic of tapping into your inner wisdom.

When you meditate, even if it's twenty to thirty minutes a day, the prefrontal cortex region in your brain is activated. It thickens, and that makes you more immune to disease. It also slows the aging process and makes you live longer. This impacts cognitive functions such as sensory and emotional processing. Regular meditation actually increases your brain capacity, and science has proven that it causes significant physiological changes that reflect greater happiness and health.

To know you're breathing right, cup your hands over your belly. You should feel it rising as you breathe in and falling as you breathe out. If you can't, then try it lying on your back so you can be more aware of your breathing pattern. Imagine your belly is a balloon getting bigger and smaller with your breath. Usually our breathing is shallow because it comes from the chest. Just the act of breathing deeper alkalizes our body. The benefits of alkalinity for your body are beyond what I can cover in this book.

If you are a total beginner, here's another way for you to try meditation. As you inhale, count from one to four very slowly, and as you exhale, count at the same speed from one to five. Then repeat. As you relax more, you will find that your inhalations and exhalations will get long enough that you can count from one to ten or even fifteen. Always try to make the exhalations a bit longer than the inhalations. This way you know you're totally emptying the air from your lungs so you're ready to take in a new batch of oxygen and nourish every cell in your body with it. When you feel you have the hang of it, try doing the same exercise, but add a one- or two-second pause in breathing at the end of every breath in and out.

When we fully connect with ourselves and learn to be present and to control the chatter in our heads, we tap into a different source of wisdom in our life. We will start to hear a new inner voice. You can call this inner voice intuition, inner wisdom, the voice of God, spiritual guidance, universal knowledge, or whatever you want. Accessing it is such a blessing.

Meditation is the perfect antidote to anxiety, nervousness, needless drama, addictions, feelings of guilt. The list goes on. In her book *Thrive: The Third Metric to Redefining Success and Creating a Life of Well-Being, Wisdom, and Wonder*, Arianna Huffington explains how burnout, stress, and depression have become worldwide epidemics. Burnout is costing Germany up to €10 billion per year. In the United Kingdom, prescriptions for antidepressants have risen 495 percent since 1991. More than twenty-two million people in the United States use illegal drugs, and more than twelve million are on painkillers without any medical reason.

As you meditate, your mind will wander off. That's normal, and that's where most people give up. Gently escort your mind back to the present moment, and continue to meditate. When it wanders off again, gently escort it back to here and now.

Relief from daily pressures is achieved simply by learning how not to emotionally overreact to the day's events. This you learn through meditation. Mindfulness-based cognitive therapy lowered the risk of depression relapse in participants from 78 percent to 36 percent[14]. Meditation is a wonder drug, but it does need to be regularly refilled, says Arriana Huffington.

Let me tell you a story I read about in several books[15] and heard mentioned in several workshops I've attended in the past. It's a story about a little town called Roseto in Pennsylvania that puzzled heart attack researchers back in the 1950s when heart attacks were an epidemic in the United

States. The residents had a lower incidence of heart attack than those in comparable towns. This is despite the fact that they broke every health rule in the book, like consuming large amounts of fatty foods, alcohol, and meat and barely exercising. Researchers dug deeper, only to find that the close family and community ties, as well as the low social competitiveness level, were the reason why the residents died of old age only. Research also showed that people with few social ties had two to five times higher mortality rates than those who had more ties. You hear it all the time: people worry about dying alone. If you have friends and strong relationships, then dying alone is less likely to happen, and dying is more likely to happen later than sooner.

In contrast to Roseto, Hurricane Katrina devastated New Orleans, Louisiana, in August 2005. In the first three months of 2006, the New Orleans Health Department reported that the state's death rate of 14.3 per 1,000 people topped the national mortality rate of 8.1 per 1,000. What this meant was that five months after the storm, people were still dying of cardiac conditions, the root cause being broken hearts or grief. Feelings of loss, grief, sorrow, and sadness over losing a loved one impact our physical states and weaken our immune systems. This causes so much stress on the heart's normal condition, chest pains follow and then cardiac arrest.

Our emotional distress manifests in a body part related to one of the seven chakras. Any illness starts with an emotion that began with a thought. Thoughts become things, and some of these things manifest in our bodies. How we spend our time thinking about life becomes how we feel about it day to day and how our life will be. Our state of consciousness determines our physical state.

Through meditation, you also improve how you react to others because you now can differentiate between you and your emotions and your stories. You effortlessly start to enjoy positive results because now your mind is uncluttered. It's in the here and now. You're tuned into positivity and solution-oriented thinking that's free from emotional baggage. This you learn through meditation when you make it a regular part of your daily routine.

Research mentioned in *Thrive* shows that you are three times more likely to be more compassionate toward others if you meditate regularly than if you don't. Imagine if these findings were taken seriously and the impact that would occur if meditation was implemented in school systems. We would create a major shift just through the simple act of teaching our young to meditate and therefore feel compassionate and caring enough to grow into social entrepreneurs seeking to cooperate and wanting to do their part in solving the world's problems.

The only case where there would be no need for meditation would be if each moment of your day, whatever you are doing, you do it fully present. You do it 100 percent. You do it like it's the only thing that matters in life. Brushing your teeth, washing your face, dressing up, tidying your bed, feeding your pet—every single simple thing you do during the day, do it mindfully. If you are sitting, sit, and if you are walking, walk. Do nothing else in that moment but the one task you are doing in that moment. I often ask my clients to do this in the morning and to do their regular routine at half the speed they usually do. Very eye-opening. Try it for yourself.

Meditation is your ticket to overcome stress, fear, and pain. It's serious business. I've engaged in it on and off since I was around twenty years old. However, since my trip to Thailand in 2017, where we had to meditate for an hour every morning as part of yoga-teacher training, I haven't stopped since. It's now a nonnegotiable way for me to start my morning, and it most definitely sets the tone for the day.

People who describe themselves as more grateful tend to be more optimistic, suffer less stress, and experience less clinical depression than the population as a whole, according to studies. Through meditation, you learn to experience more gratitude. This is the antidote to negative emotions like entitlement and anger. Just think about this for a minute. If you are reading this book, that means you can read, which means you are most probably educated or highly educated. You definitely have a roof over your head and a warm bed for sleeping. Maybe you're already reading in bed, feeling bloated after a big meal, and you have a hot cup of tea (the water for which you boiled using an electric kettle) on your bedside table that has a table lamp on it so you can read, which means you also have running electricity. You are winding down after a day at work, so you have a job or your own business, or you just put the kids to bed and are enjoying some me time. Or maybe you are reading at the beach after an exhausting Zumba class at your gym. Whatever it may be, I hope you realize that you should be grateful for the million little things you already have. Bless your life every day by counting your blessings daily. When we forget to be humble and grateful, we become arrogant. We take from Mother Earth and from one another with a sense of entitlement. We destroy all that is green and blue and pollute the air we breathe.

Mother Teresa refused the traditional banquet offered at Nobel Peace Prize events. Instead, she asked that all the money that would have been spent on the event go toward feeding the poor. That's humility for you that comes with awareness, and with awareness, we make more conscious and mindful decisions.

You Are What You Eat

There are three words that convey the secret of the art of living, the secret of all success and happiness: One With Life. Being one with life is being one with Now. You then realize that you don't live your life, but life lives you. Life is the dancer, and you are the dance.

—Eckhart Tolle, *A New Earth: Awakening to Your Life's Purpose*

We need energy to survive, and our bodies get that energy from any source around us: good food, bad food, the environment, and even from other people's energies, which are also called vibes. If we spend more energy than we receive, we experience burnout. So let's talk a little bit about what we feed our body.

We need hydrogen and oxygen (H_2O, the chemical elements of water) to fully take in the nourishment from our food. We often feel hungry when, in fact, all our body needs at that moment is water.

HALT is an acronym that originated in addiction rehabilitation programs. It's a good way to measure what you are experiencing when you want to attack your fridge around midnight when nobody else is watching, especially after committing to a healthy lifestyle and proper eating habits. HALT stands for Hungry, Angry, Lonely, or Tired. And you might as well add another *T* at the end for Thirsty. Ask yourself if you are feeling any of those emotions, and address them accordingly instead of addressing them by unnecessarily stuffing your face.

The thyroid is all about planning and communication. Adrenaline is the driving force that helps us get things done. Cortisol, a hormone released in response to stress and low blood sugar levels, is the creative high-power state that cools off stress so the body can achieve things. When we learn to skillfully and simultaneously combine the best traits of the thyroid, adrenaline, and cortisol in our bodies, we are maximizing the positive use of hormonal energy to create a good life.

The following is a list of some hormones and how high or low levels of them affect our moods and our bodies.

· Serotonin: When it is high, you feel positive, confident, flexible, and easygoing. Otherwise, you feel negative, obsessive, worried, irritable, and sleepless.

- Catecholamines (norepinephrine, dopamine, and adrenaline are in this group): When they are high, you feel energized, upbeat, and alert. Otherwise, you feel flat and in a lethargic funk.

- Gamma aminobutyric acid: When it is high, you feel relaxed and stress-free. Otherwise, you feel wired, stressed, and overwhelmed.

- Endorphins: When they are high, they give you that cozy feeling of comfort, pleasure, and euphoria. Otherwise, you'll find yourself crying during commercials and overly sensitive to hurtful things.

Ongoing anxiety and irritation, mood swings, lack of proper sleep, and constant aches and pains all cause stress on the body. Stress magnifies leptin problems, and weight gain is a common consequence. Nutritionist Byron J. Richards calls leptin the CEO of all hormones in *The Leptin Diet*, a book that I recommend you read, even though I'm not big on reading nutrition books as each one tells you not to do what another book tells you to do.

To prevent disease, we have to have the proper amount of each hormone. But how do we make sure that we do this? Here are the five rules of the leptin diet and for optimal health[16]:

1. Never eat after dinner.

2. Eat three meals a day.

3. Don't eat large meals.

4. Eat a breakfast containing protein.

5. Reduce carbohydrates.

Studies conducted at the University of California–Los Angeles found that two-thirds of people who go on a diet gain back more weight than they initially lost within four or five years. With such a gloomy outcome, a higher happiness set point provides a much-needed boost. It convinces us that our weight-loss goal is achievable. It fortifies our resolve to resist temptations along the way. Studies further indicated that dieters who showed an optimistic attitude by setting higher weight-loss goals and expressing greater confidence in the attainment of those goals actually did lose more weight.

I often post to my Instagram as I prepare what I call the breakfast of champions. It's my famous shake. I get more questions about it than I get about life coaching. Here's what I put in it that makes it so nutritious. I'm not a nutritionist nor claim to be, but this is what I do for myself, and you are free to do your own research before deciding to give my shake a try.

1. Use a nondairy milk. Turns out only cows should drink cow milk. So, I use almond, soy, rice, or coconut milk.

2. Add a banana or some fresh berries. Any kind of berry is a good antioxidant for the body.

3. Add half an avocado. Avocados are fatty, yes, but when consumed in the morning, your body knows to

use them up for energy, so it's good fat that you burn throughout the day. Same applies to the spoonful of coconut oil I mix with my coffee in the morning.

4. Add a tablespoonful or two of chia-and-flaxseeds mix. Let me not get started on their benefits; I will not finish this book if I do. Suffice it to say that the word *chia* means *strength*. Chia is a seed that's used as an energy booster because it contains omega-3, protein, carbohydrates, fiber, and antioxidants. It's your one-stop shop. And flaxseed is great because it makes you feel full, has loads of fiber, and also contains omega-3, which is good for your heart.

5. Add a teaspoon of wheatgrass. That's like adding 92 out of more than 102 minerals found in soil, and 17 amino acids, including the 8 essential amino acids that they body cannot manufacture by itself. In that teaspoon you are also enjoying the benefits of vitamins A, B, C and E. That's not to mention that it also includes chlorophyll and a lot of enzymes.

After this shake, I'm good to go till lunch and feel like I've treated my body to total goodness. There you have it. Doesn't it sound like a breakfast of champions to you? Just think of food as a form of self-love and your kitchen a source of that love. Mindfully choose how you want to express love for your body and all it does for you.

It takes twenty minutes for your body to signal that it's full, so eating mindfully allows you time for the signaling to happen. Plus, you eat less and enjoy more.

And whatever you do, don't forget to drink water. Water constitutes 75 percent of your brain, 75 percent of your muscles, and 22 percent of your bones. Hydration is super important, and we often underestimate what happens to our bodies when we don't have enough of it. Just by hydrating your body consistently, you are helping your cells absorb nutrients and oxygen, regulate your body temperature, convert food to energy, remove bodily waste, and cushion your vital organs and joints. Simply sipping a bit of water throughout the day helps keep your lymphatic system in tip-top condition. And the lymphatic system is the one that radically impacts all the other systems. It's how your body cleans itself. Add a slice of lemon to your water, and now you also alkalize your body while you hydrate it. Win-win all the way!

Boosting Your Self-Image

The significant problems we face cannot be solved at the same level of thinking with which we created them.

—Albert Einstein

Tony Robbins explains at his seminars how you can shift your state or blueprint on the spot. Your state—or how you are feeling at the moment—changes all the time. Three forces determine that change.

1. Patterns of physiology: How you use your physical body, such as breath, posture, movement; how your body is built; etcetera.

2. Patterns of focus: Whatever you focus on, you will feel. What you focus on depends on your values, your rules for fulfilling those values, and your global beliefs, all which constitute your identity.

3. Patterns of language/meaning: As soon as we attach words to an experience, it changes the meaning of what we experience. The words we attach to an experience are related to the questions we habitually ask ourselves, the metaphors we habitually use, and the belief systems we apply to ourselves, such as "I'm not enough," "I can't do anything right," or "I'm very smart."

Change any one of these forces, and you can shift your state in an instant.

Who in your life do you most love and admire? For the longest time, it was my baby sister Reem. She's funny, smart, loving, adorable, giving, caring, and wants to help others and the world. She's creative, artistic, a fast learner, beautiful, determined, and overcomes her own challenges. Notice how all these things are not physical? They are not about the body. And notice how much time we spend worrying about the body and how we look and what we wear?

By the way, all the attributes I listed that I love about her are attributes that are also within myself. I may just be unaware of them, or they are attributes that I want to be mine, so I aspire toward them. Find examples of how that's true for you. Everything you love about someone is you. It's what you love about yourself. And you'll find that only very few characteristics, if any, are related to body size and shape.

And God said, "Love your Enemy." And I obeyed him and loved myself.

—Khalil Gibran

Even our worst enemies don't talk to us the way we talk to ourselves in our heads and in front of the mirror. Our self-talk is full of poisonous words that fill us with insecurity and doubt. Excess weight is almost always indicative of deeper problems. Our insecurities make us want to protect or shield ourselves from others, and we do it subconsciously with a layer of fat. The more insecure we are, the thicker the layers. Anorexia and bulimia are extreme expressions of a lack of self-love. How can there be self-love when there's so much self-judgment?

What we need is a mental diet. A cleanse of all the negative mental shit we harbor in our minds and of the poisonous words we make ourselves believe to be true. Go on a diet from negative thoughts and self-talk, and watch your body lose weight on its own. A daily cleanse of your emotional waste is a must, just like you dispose of physical body wastes and toxins and how you throw out your garbage at home. You do this by not going to bed angry and by not letting any unfinished emotional business linger. This is how you are cleansed of noise and become ready to hear the voice of your intuition. And learn from it, respond to it, and honor it.

For some, this concept is very hard. How do we love ourselves? How do we not love ourselves? No matter what the problem, the root cause is lack of self-love. Each one of us has a value, and that value is determined by how much you love and honor yourself. If you don't like someone, you walk away from them, but if you don't like yourself, there's nowhere to go, so your only option is self-love. Don't take yourself for granted!

Just think about this for a second. All your life, you've been feeding yourself, nourishing yourself, clothing yourself, bathing yourself. So, all this time, you've been taking care of you and doing a great job of it. This is the longest lasting relationship you've ever had and ever will have.

In other words, this means I am in a relationship with myself. We all are in a relationship with ourselves. In Ireland, when I was celebrating turning forty, I had tears running down my face as I realized that I was in love with myself. I give myself all I need to be entertained, happy, clothed, well-traveled, nourished, pampered, and more. It's got nothing to do with a man or other people around me. I've learned to see the fire, tenacity, kindness, compassion, strength, and resilience in myself. I don't need someone else to remind me of that.

This is a letter I wrote to myself during one of the workshops I attended a few years back. I invite you to write one for yourself.

My dear body,

I love your hands, your fingers, your arms. I never noticed how beautiful you are. Thank you belly for how soft and curved you are. I love touching you. Thank you feet for taking me to all the places you did. Thanks for the pain and I am sorry for not listening earlier. Sorry that you had to suffer because I was ignorant or stubborn. I apologize for not looking at you earlier. For not seeing that all I needed was to look inside for all my answers. That the heart you shelter is my guide and the one to point me in the right direction. I will appreciate you more going forward. I promise. I will listen to the signs and watch out for you. My beautiful spine, I love you. You've supported me even when you were collapsed. You allowed me to do what I had to do even when I was bent over with pain. I will not be ashamed of you. You and I are the perfect partners. Sorry for stuffing you with food beyond your comfort zone. I love you for processing all the acne and pimples and the torture I made my face go through. Thank you for healing those scars from all the pimples I squeezed till my face bled. Thank you for getting me to thirty-six as beautifully as you've done. Thank you for feeling your energy and the energy of beautiful things around us and the ugly things around us so I can protect you from the bad and go closer to the good. Thank you for carrying my

> head even when I gave you shit. I will love you more. I will pat you and stroke you. I love you for being so forgiving of all I've done to you and the verbal abuse. Next time I get a compliment about you, I will not brush it off, I will say thank you. Going forward we'll take better care of one another. I see the goddess in you and I honor you. Thank you. I love you.

What gets in the way of self-love is self-criticism. Stop criticizing yourself. Stop saying you're always "too" something. Too fat, too skinny, too stupid, too blond, too short. Stop saying the biggest lie of all—that you're not good enough.

We're all pretty good at criticizing ourselves. We've done it for decades and have become pros. And if you take a moment to notice, you'll realize that didn't work for you. Try loving yourself and your body. Unconditionally. As is. People who do are more compassionate, caring, and loving to others as well. Any issue my clients come to me with is because of one root cause: not enough self-love. Be like babies, who are perfect with all their chubby hips and bulging bellies. They act like they know how perfect and lovable they are!

Would you tell a five-year-old that she's stupid, fat, or not good enough? If you did, she'd either lose all sense of identity and become insecure, or she'd rebel and wreck the place. That's what you do to yourself.

Exercise

Write out this phrase and complete it, as many times as it takes, until your hand is sore from writing: "I love and approve of myself, therefore ______."

Going forward, try to make your time in front of the mirror a time to gain points with yourself again. So let's be mindful of our vocabulary while we talk with ourselves in front of the mirror.

First of all, don't ever say you "should" do or be anything. You should nothing. In a bouquet of flowers, one flower doesn't look at the others and say, "I'm not big enough," "I'm not red like her," "I don't smell strong enough." Each flower is just what it is. For a change, be a flower!

On the other hand, you "could" do and be a lot of things. The difference is that with the word *could*, you are opening a world of choice and opportunity for your mind instead of the dictatorship energy of *should*!

Every time you say, "I should," stop yourself and ask why. Exchange that with "If I really wanted to, I could …" Do you notice the difference in the energy of these two options? Even as I type them, I can feel the difference. In the first option, I'm feeling bullied. In the second, I'm feeling empowered.

The power and heavy load that some words carry can be paralyzing, and we don't even notice their effect on us until it's seemingly too late. If I hold up a glass of water with my arm stretched out, how heavy that glass is depends on how long I hold it. If I hold it for a minute, that's not a problem. If I hold it for an hour, I'll have an ache in my arm. If I hold it for a day, you'll have to call an ambulance. In each case, it's the same weight, but the longer I hold it, the heavier it becomes.

If we carry our burdens or stress all the time, with no help or no break, sooner or later, we will collapse with exhaustion and with symptoms that will manifest physically. But like the glass of water, if you can put your troubles down for a while and rest before picking them up again, you will go further. When you stop to take care of your well-being—heart, mind, body, and soul—your burdens won't seem so heavy or cumbersome.

A good way to notice your thought patterns is to write them down. After a while, have a look at them, and you will be able to see your patterns in black and white. Then become a nasty, nosy private investigator. Interrogate each and every one of those thoughts. Ask if it is true; think of examples of when that thought has actually occurred and ask when it last happened. Dig deeper and deeper with your questioning until you laugh at yourself. You will notice how you make up stories and worry about things that never happened. Some of the stress-inducing thought patterns that we commonly have are:

- all-or-nothing thinking

- overgeneralization

- biased mental filtering of the whole story

- jumping to conclusions

- magnification

- minimalization

- seeking approval

- self-righteousness

Every day, girls are being exposed to unrealistic standards of beauty. A lot of people in the entertainment business and fashion industry have eating disorders. A girl can be born plain, but if she believes herself to be gorgeous, she can be the sexiest woman in the room.

Our sense of self-esteem starts to develop early in life. We begin with a clean slate, but it gets junked up fast. In every stage in your life, people come along who test your self-esteem. There's always going to be someone who is going to try to tear you down. Self-love is something we have to work hard at every day. Anyone who says she's confident 100 percent of the time is either lying or delusional. It's okay to have ups and downs. Hell is here and now, and so is heaven. Every time we love, we are in heaven, and every time we don't, we are in hell—a hell of our own doing. I asked a friend who was struggling with self-love to write, "You are beautiful," on her mirror. She told me she couldn't and wouldn't do it. It's that same mirror she allows to tell her every day that she's old and has wrinkles!

Women excel at tearing one another down. Men aren't nearly as complicated. If they like you, they'll hang out with you; if they don't, they won't. Women can be so competitive with one another, and it stems from insecurity and not enough self-love. Be selective with whom you associate. Clean up your contacts list to match your life of well-being.

When something is wrong with your knee, it's okay to go see someone to fix it. When something is wrong with your emotional well-being, it's looked down on to seek help. "Suck it up" is most likely the suggestion you get. When you are feeling stress, it's not considered a biggie. Just take Tylenol and sleep it off, or maybe have some molten chocolate lava cake! So we lock it all inside, and it makes us ill as it goes unattended for a long time.

Remember that you are the witness of it all. You are not your feelings. You are not the thought. You are not the emotions. You are the witness. Your consciousness focuses on where you put your attention. If you don't stay connected to your core and the essence of who you truly are, your attention will be scattered, and you will forget how to be centered —how to be you. Not having any thoughts is not a solution. There will always be thoughts, and we have to find freedom from reacting to every single one of them as they keep coming. That's mindfulness.

Chapter 13

Your Soul Wants to Serve

To each there comes in their lifetime a special moment when they are figuratively tapped on the shoulder and offered the chance to do a very special thing, unique to them and fitted to their talents. What a tragedy if that moment finds them unprepared or unqualified for that which could have been their finest hour.

—Sir Winston Churchill

WHAT does our soul want? The soul wants to serve something greater and bigger than the self. It wants freedom from the limitations of our physical bodies and minds. It wants to go on a quest, conquer a challenge, or leave a legacy.

Socrates defined his life's mission as awakening the Athenians to the supreme importance of attending to their souls. He said, "The unexamined life is not worth living."

Our hearts, minds, and bodies are instruments of the soul. Fixing the piano won't help a sick player. The kind of music that a pianist can produce does not depend only on the instrument but also on the state of the pianist herself. The instrument is but a tool. Our life purpose is to serve. To fulfill our soul's calling.

We want our influence and work on this planet to last way beyond the span of our own lives and to have an impact on a lot more people than just ourselves. Our souls believe in "we" more than "me." That's why some of us have big dreams and goals and want our names on buildings and books and to have inventions and patents credited to us.

The word for *soul* in Arabic is *nafs*, and in the Quran, the serene *nafs* is mentioned many times. When you get to that state of having a serene soul, you are in an altered state of consciousness. You have an unwavering sense of contentment no matter what life throws at you. This kind of state is not easy to achieve and, once gained, not easy to maintain. That's why very few ever reach it.

Death is inevitable, an indisputable fact. We are all dying on the physical level. But our deeds, impact, lifetime's work, and story will live on forever. Our soul is immortal.

A study by management professor Thomas Åstebro at the University of Toronto found that inventors are more overconfident and optimistic than the general public. More than half of the inventors in the study continued to spend time on their projects even after being told to cease effort. Why? Because it made them happy to work on something meaningful. It nourished their souls. Even if it was a vision that only they believed in! It fed their need for contribution.

We all want to serve on a scale larger than life. Once upon a time, people believed the world was flat, but one man proved them wrong. Once upon a time, people believed the moon was unreachable, but then we walked on it. Once upon a time, people thought the desert was a dead place, but now whole countries are thriving in it.

> *Every man gives his life for what he believes. Every woman gives her life for what she believes. Sometimes people believe in little or nothing, and so they give their lives to little or nothing.*

> —Joan of Arc

The world's greatest challenges and problems are those concerning people. It comes down to the individual level. Down to people like you and me. So if each one of us helps or teaches one other person who is in need, then each one of us can save one other life.

Civilization is the result of the effort of people before us who worked on projects that were essentially immortal, like Steve Jobs, Sheikh Zayed bin Sultan Al Nahyan, Mahatma Gandhi, Galileo Galilei, Pablo Picasso, Mother Teresa, Martin Luther King, Jr., and many, many others. Their work is as alive and impactful today, if not more, as it was back when they were still alive. Their work was something that they were passionate about and that clearly fulfilled their lives and gave them meaning.

> *Every individual has to perform his duty. Man is mortal, but his work is not. Therefore, work is greater than wealth.*

> — Sheikh Zayed bin Sultan Al Nahyan

Our lives do not belong to us. Whether we know it or not, we are bound to others from birth. It is through every act of kindness and love that we feel more alive and life is vibrantly colorful. When we love another person, we see the face of the divine because we are born to love and are fulfilling that purpose. Love is to be given, and to love another is the most natural way of being. It's through the act of loving someone else that the spring of love is continuously regenerating within us so there's more to give and the flow is infinite instead of stale. Funny how it works, too; the more you give, the more you have of it. It cannot be saved or hoarded for oneself. It runs through our veins, bodies, thoughts, and our very existence. To deny it is to deny life itself.

If someone were to take a sample of your core/essence, what qualities would they find? If you were to be peeled like an onion, one layer at a time, what would you find at your core? If you had an animal shadow and you portrayed the characteristics of that animal in your soul, what animal would that be?

Scott Harrison was on top of the world, living the high life while working as a nightclub promoter for ten years. His goal was to drive as many people as possible into his clubs and to get them as drunk as he could. He gambled, smoked, used drugs, had a pornography addiction—the list goes on.

Then, one night, on a private island in South America, he somehow woke up to the fact that he not only was miserable, but he was the worst person he knew. He said, "I realized the legacy I was creating, what I was going to be known for, was that guy who threw parties and got people wasted."

Disgusted, he decided a radical change was due. He needed to take stock of his life. He needed to take time to assess it; then he needed to act and get involved. That's how he discovered his passion, which became his soul's mission.

After a few weeks of this new shift in perspective, he decided to volunteer and offer his knowledge and expertise to a humanitarian organization. He contacted many and was refused. But he was relentless until he got a yes. Mercy Ships, an organization that provides floating hospitals that travel to the poorest regions of the world to offer free medical care, accepted him. His job was to be their photojournalist, capturing stories. This opportunity opened his eyes to the world of suffering that was so much the polar opposite of the life he'd been living. Upon his return to New York in 2006, he founded an organization called charity: water whose aim is to provide safe drinking water to eight hundred million people who don't have it. Now, that's his legacy.

The power of intention works in such a way that when it comes from the mind, it is weak and full of ego. You are in your head. But when it comes from the soul, it is strong and has its own mechanics to make the universe conspire along to manifest and fulfill that intention.

I believe that people are innately good. They are, by nature, compassionate and empathetic most days of the week. They may be influenced to be otherwise, but we're all born with good in our hearts. Just look at Wikipedia. The information it contains, which is crowdsourced (meaning anyone can make edits or add information), is almost as accurate as a typical article in the *Encyclopedia Britannica*! So, left to their own devices, people are good by nature and want to serve and be helpful.

When people are free to tap into their core, their essence is pure, and they do good. Just imagine how many crimes or acts of cruelty of any kind could *potentially* be committed in your very own neighborhood. Now think about how many *actually* do happen any given day or month or year. The ratio, according to Daniel Goleman, is close to zero any day of the year[17].

Tapping into Something Bigger Than You

We who lived in concentration camps can remember the men who walked through the huts comforting others, giving away their last piece of bread. They may have been few in number, but they offer sufficient proof that everything can be taken from a man but one thing: the last of the human freedoms—to choose one's attitude in any given set of circumstances, to choose one's own way.

—Viktor E. Frankl

My father's philosophy in life is, "If you can give, you should." He grew up poor but told me he never felt poor.

He grew up grateful for everything he did have, working hard for what he wanted. He instilled in me a deep desire to serve and the gift of gratitude for every little blessing this universe gives me.

Why are we taught that it is better to give than to receive? Why exactly does it feel so good when we give to others? Are there benefits to giving as a chosen lifestyle? Why should this be taught in schools and instilled in our children from an early age?

Giving has many forms, of course. It can be monetary, but more importantly, it can be giving of a far more valuable asset: your time. Money is something you can make back, but time, once spent, never comes back.

Thomas Sander, executive director of the Saguaro Seminar at the John F. Kennedy School of Government at Harvard University, said, "Civic engagement and volunteering is the new hybrid health club for the twenty-first century that's free to join. Social capital research shows it miraculously improves both your health and the community's through the work performed and the social ties built."

One of the biggest and most obvious benefits of volunteering is the impact it has on the community. Unpaid volunteers are often the glue that holds a community together. But another less obvious benefit is how much connection it gives you—to your community, to friends with common interests, to family members who volunteer with you, and to yourself.

Research at the London School of Economics from 2008 shows there's a huge positive emotional impact of volunteerism on the volunteer. By giving, you are actually receiving way more. Self-esteem increases as your social and team-building skills develop, and you feel you have an important role and a sense of pride, accomplishment, and identity. People who frequently volunteer even advance in their careers as a consequence of all the skills they learn through volunteering. Even thinking about helping others boosts our health because it increases the level of immunoglobulin A, an antibody that defends against disease, in our body. Symptoms of depression also decrease because you are thinking less about yourself and more about becoming an important part of the solution for another person or community in need. Psychotherapists even suggest volunteering as a depression-combating mechanism. It has also been linked to longevity and improving the quality of lives of the elderly, even when they do things as simple as feeding little rescue kittens. Lastly, your physical health improves all in all, and people who volunteer have a higher mortality rate.

As if all that were not enough, helping others increases happiness levels, as many studies have demonstrated. When researchers at the London School of Economics examined the relationship between volunteering and measures of happiness in a large group of adults, they found that the more people volunteered, the happier they were. Compared with people who never volunteered, the odds of being very happy rose 7 percent among those who volunteered monthly, 12 percent for people who volunteered every two to four weeks, and 16 percent for those who volunteered on a weekly basis.

My Wake-Up Call in India

If anyone saved a life, it would be as if he saved the life of all mankind.

—Quran 5:32

Your soul is the very essence of what makes you *you*. Ignore your soul and you suffocate. Your soul is the medium connecting you to your higher self, to the universal wisdom, to God. Your soul takes care of everything beyond what your physical body can do. Spirituality is experienced only when you are tapped into your soul and truly connected to it, and therefore tapped into every other soul. Consciousness is measured by whom (and how many people) you care about. This goes beyond just your family!

Feel-good hormones like serotonin, oxytocin, endorphins, and dopamine are released when a person sees a direct, positive result from their volunteer work. The act of being of service and exchanging positive energy with another human is a psychological and emotional win-win.

Your life is a direct reflection of the expectations of your team. By *team*, I'm referring to the five or six people you are in constant touch with. Think about this for a second: if you merge those five or six people into one person, that person would be you. You, with all the good, the bad, and the ugly! So open your horizons a bit more. Stretch the limit and extend yourself to those beyond immediate family and friends. Open your world. Let *team* mean a community, a nation, or even humanity. The sky is the limit.

I had a pretty stressful time a few years back because of some family issues as well as being overwhelmed from working seven days a week for many months in a row, and I kept saying that I needed to slow down. I would say the words to myself but still go about life at full speed. I would even verbalize wanting to slow the engines down to the point where I could see the engine fans, but I kept going full throttle.

My stress level was getting higher and higher. Until I woke up one morning with crazy foot pain. Sparing you the details, I ended up having to go to the doctor for a small procedure. Of course, I was forced to walk extremely slowly because of the pain caused whenever I put my foot down to walk.

I got it! I got the message loud and clear. I just had to have this incredible pain in my foot to hear it and finally slow down. I was so out of touch with my soul that this intervention had to happen. The universe had to step in!

This coincided with a friend suggesting that I join her at a spiritual course she was attending in India that was only five days away. She sent me the link, and within forty-eight hours, I had registered, got myself a visa, and bought my airline ticket. India was calling. I had to go.

I arrived late in the evening, had a bumpy three-hour taxi ride to the resort south of Chennai, got myself checked in, closed the door after the bellboy walked out, and turned around to see the most beautiful wooden fan on the ceiling with ribs shaped like palm leaves. It was very symbolic of the engine fans I had wanted to slow down, and I just thought,

Yes, I can be parked out here for a while. My life slowed down considerably from then on.

If we don't slow down, how can we see the truth? How can we see what is really going on with our lives and where we are heading when we are going at full speed?

My favorite way to listen to my higher self or to feel tapped into the universal source of knowing is to focus on areas where I need guidance and write them down or just meditate on a question last thing before I go to bed and make sure it is the very last activity of the day. Then I fall asleep and let the answers flow through my dreams. When I wake up, I start a free flow of writing down everything I dreamed, starting with the things I wrote down the night before.

Try this. You will notice a new sense of awareness rising. It will be like you are finding your own answers. It's as if you are looking at the problem from a completely new perspective or through a completely new lens. Ask for answers in the evening, and listen to the answers in the morning. The key is that you have to be open to all and any signs showing you these answers. The sign can be a concrete thing like receiving a letter or a phone call, or it can be abstract, like simply having a confident resolve about your next step. You have to be curious about answers or signs you don't understand. Be curious and be patient. Keep asking.

The answers to all your questions already reside inside you —not in your mind but in your soul. There's no question/problem that you don't have the answer/solution for. So you must be able to trust yourself and have the ability to quiet yourself and let the answers emerge.

Journaling, freewriting, stream of consciousness—whatever you like to call it—is a powerful tool to gain clarity, process emotions and thoughts, and receive great insight. Write three full pages without stopping to edit, censor, or daydream. Don't let your pen leave the page, and keep it flowing. If you get really stuck, write, "What I really want to say is ..." and finish the sentence.

Writing down your thoughts, worries, experiences, and happiness is therapeutic. Journaling can boost immunity, reduce illnesses, relieve pain, and decrease depression and anxiety. Handwriting your thoughts is the best way to go about it. There's something magical about putting thoughts down to paper. It puts your problems and issues into perspective and makes decision-making easier. It's the safest way to explore the dark side of you and your negative emotions. But it's also an incredible way to celebrate the triumphs and experience gratitude.

Here's a sample of journal entries I wrote a few years back during a nine-day course, Byron Katie's "The School for the Work." As part of the program, we went for a daily morning walk before breakfast and were asked to just name whatever we saw using the simplest form of description, one word. I made note of my thoughts afterward. I'm sharing them here to show you how much you can discover about yourself and learn just by writing your thoughts down on paper.

> Journal entry, March 25
>
> As I did the morning walk, I came to the awareness that everything has several names to it if you speak several languages and there is no right or

wrong name. It's the same with every thought, belief and idea … they can have different meanings or interpretations or ways of looking at them. There is no right or wrong. Then I got very distracted and wanted to just focus on the walk itself, so I kept repeating "step after step" to myself.

Journal entry, March 25

I don't need to name everything I come in touch with. I don't need to necessarily attach a label to everything. They are all just things. So taking this into my life would be that I don't need to attach an emotion or a feeling to events that happen to me. I don't even have to be hooked and attached to what I always believed to be true.

Journal entry, March 26

I was determined to get the exercise right. So I started renaming things out of a dictionary. I switched names of objects I'm seeing and then decided I'm going to go with simplicity. So company became idea. A car became carriage. A plant became seed. Then I saw a homeless guy sleeping on a bench with his hoodie covering his head and I felt sad. I saw the blind woman in our group stopping to smell the flowers. The same flowers I wanted to go smell but didn't because I wanted to keep walking. Slow down and appreciate it all … that is the message I got. The homeless guy was still there on the way back and I tried just loving what is. He's there because of a sequence of choices or life events and he's just where he needs to be, having a nap. Loving what is. I saw a man with 2 prosthetic legs. The other blind woman in our group yesterday stood up to tell us that we are all beautiful to her. A blind woman can see the beauty in us that we (who can see) fail to. At breakfast I was thinking that when I thought I just had too much love in me, Byron Katie just taught me that I can love even more, I can love even that which I fear the most then I thought of dad and me worrying about him and that made me cry. Loving what is … there is no other way to live. It is what it is.

Journal entry, March 27

I cheated last night and went online to check some emails. I got no reply to my last email to my boyfriend and I received an email regarding that investment property I had. And I got myself all too upset. So this morning, I went into the walk feeling angry. Last night I didn't manage to let go of some prejudices in one of the exercises they took us through and I had a conversation with my roommate that triggered all sorts of shit regarding my marriage and ex-husband. So all in all, I had all I need for an angry walk. I was in my stories. The homeless guy was triggering more anger. I wanted to poke him and ask if he was staged. Did someone pay him to sit there in the same spot in the same position. Then I forced myself to follow the simple instructions and I was stomping. My thoughts are killing me. They spiral me downward. My thoughts will be the death of me. I decided to be "silent one" for the day and sink into this to see what comes up.

Journal entry, March 28

I walked with Joanne today. I asked her yesterday if I can volunteer to walk her and she said yes gladly. Joanne is blind. I asked her if she needs me to describe to her the steps and sidewalks etc., and she said: "No need, if you hesitate, I will notice and I'll figure it out!" That made my walk! The turnaround story was in my head throughout the walk. If I hesitate I will notice and I will figure it out. Then I noticed the lady with bone problems who shared yesterday that she was taking extra pills to catch up with us and I decided I want to walk with her tomorrow. I want to help others. No one left behind. I want to give of myself to others and I feel nourished doing so. I need to take care of myself while doing that because people come first, and if I forget myself I don't serve others as well.

Journal entry, March 29

I took a route this morning that was all concrete. So I was thinking concrete, concrete, concrete.

Didn't feel like renaming things. I saw all as love. So I started saying concrete, love, concrete, love. Then it became Concrete Love. And I loved that. So I saw love in everything. The greenery to soften the scene. The soft toys in the RAM truck. The soft toy on a car's antennae. Metal van said HOME. Another car had food under it. It was all love and I can't have enough of it and I can't give enough. I want to love and love and love.

Journal entry, March 30

I felt like a horse waiting for the door at a race to open so that I can bolt out. The route was all planes, buses, and cars. I wanted to run. I was right next to our guide and it felt like he's walking too slow for me today. I feel unstoppable and ready to march forward with my plans. My mind is already in the future.

Journal entry, March 31

I kept trying to sink into the work. During meditation I was thinking that I always want to blend in and be quiet when what I really want to do is whip up a storm. I want to be loud. I want to smash stuff. Make a stink. Break some glass. But I always hush myself because there's no time for a tantrum. Ever since I had my two younger siblings come into my life, I felt like I need to protect them and help them and be there for them. So I put myself last. Always did. As if I am not important and I don't matter. Then I get upset at the whole world and I rebelled all these years. Until I was a ball of anger, a timed bomb and became an outcast. I had to leave. Packed everything and started a new life so far away from them all. Was I running away from myself?

Awakening: A State of Bliss

If you plan on being anything less than you are capable of, you will probably be unhappy all the days of your life.

—Abraham Maslow

The soul wants to play larger than life. The soul does not want to be caged in your comfort zone, no matter how comfortable it is. Spiritual awakening is realizing how small that cage is and waking up to the big wide world out there.

You can be in one of two states of being. You can be aware—conscious—which is a state of joy, love, and peace, a state that expands your soul. Or you can be unaware—unconscious—which is a state of suffering that shrinks your soul.

You find your way from the state of suffering to a state of joy from within. All suffering is the fabrication of the mind. False beliefs and assumptions are your superhighway into darkness and a state of unawareness. And we blindly hang on to them.

We assume that suffering is a challenge or a problem. Not true. Challenges and problems are external and always have a solution. We assume suffering is pain. Not true. Pain is physical. Suffering is internal. It is mental. Suffering is your thoughts. It is also self-centered. Your thoughts surrounding suffering are all about you. You don't suffer for someone else. You suffer only for yourself. Yes, you feel compassion for another person and care about them, but when you suffer, it's about the self. We assume that suffering is a blessing, and we create a whole persona around it. Like it's a gift bestowed on you from high above. Blessings cause you to feel gratitude—even when they come with tears—because you view the situation now from a positive perspective, like it's a lesson. Blessings don't cause suffering unless you are unaware.

Another more common word for suffering is *stress*. Stress caused by other people or situations. That's also not a true assumption. If we suffer from events in our life, it is not about the event; it's about how we think of it in our state of unawareness. If you believe suffering is your destiny; that it's karma; if you say, "It's the story of my life"; that it's God's gift to you; or anything along those lines, then that's *no bueno*. It is merely an attempt to deflect your responsibility to do the right thing to try to end your suffering. It causes inaction. No action means no transformation. It renders you useless! Then you're trapped in a poor-me mentality, and in that state, how can you ever be in the mood to allow your soul to serve? In that state, you are so absorbed in poor you and only you.

I find myself repeatedly telling my clients that they don't have to tell me the whole story with all its nitty-gritty details. The stories are always either exaggerated or diluted. It all depends on who's doing the telling. The story, therefore, doesn't matter. It's not that I don't care. It's just that what matters more and what I'd like to know is how it made them feel. What did they make that story mean? How did they react? But there seems to be a pressing need to continue with their story's details because they want me to understand how much they are suffering as a consequence or how much of a victim they are and that their story is different from anybody else's, so by providing all the details, they expect the solution for them will be a different one. Not true. It's the same way out of the darkness for us all. To open your eyes and to ask yourself my favorite question of all: What don't I see?

The difference between a person who is aware and another who is not is the level of awareness they bring to their emotions as they surface. Do you sit with that emotion? Or do you distract yourself with any of the two dozen obsessions you have created in your life to avoid dealing with your emotions and what's really happening inside? What is your habitual reaction every time you feel stressed? Notice. Now that's the most important word in the dictionary: *notice*! I have probably mentioned this before, but it is worth repeating. To notice is a very important thing.

Here's what I noticed that I do. I live with it. My pain threshold is so high, I tolerate more than I really want to.

Then I get angry and sometimes explode. I wait, and I hate waiting. So it makes me feel even more anger. Then I get tired of the anger and the waiting and indulge in self-pity. Or I decide to go on an unaware-thinking roller-coaster ride that doesn't end. It just loops over and over again. Then I get tired of that, so I distract myself with my goals. Or I decide to sleep the whole thing off. I also procrastinate. And sometimes I just indulge in useless distractions that help me run away from dealing with or thinking about what's really going on with me. And sometimes I deflect the anger onto some other poor soul who happens to cross my path that day. Immediately after, I wallow in guilt and self-hate for being so mean or cruel or cold, and it goes on and on and on …

How can clarity come when there's confusion? Suffering causes a confused state of mind. In my example above, it's a stupid state of mind, not an intelligent one. In the process of unaware thinking, you are creating more and more distance between you and the people you love, and you move further and further away from a solution, one that comes from awareness. You become disconnected from your soul and totally engrossed in your ego.

We can't have one state without the other. Just like day and night, one has to exist so we can appreciate the other. I get it. However, we need to wake up to the truth so we can spend less time suffering and spend more time basking in joy, peace, and love. Say amen to that!

Okay, now you may be asking, "How do we wake up and become aware?" Awareness is not the absence of thoughts, and it's not about exchanging one bad thought for a good thought. Thoughts rarely appear solo. It's always like a swarm of bees. They come all at once. They are like magnets making your attention snap back to an old memory or sad event in the past, making this thought pattern no different from an addiction to smoking or drinking. Moreover, it is almost sadistic to keep doing that to yourself.

To wake up and end your suffering, you need to do three things:

1. Recognize your suffering. Name it. Be specific and don't undermine it.

2. Observe your thoughts. Find the pattern of how you react to them. Do you blame, project, make up stories, invest so much meaning into everything, overanalyze? Ask about the truth behind it all. Ask, "What don't I see?"

3. Realize that your experience of suffering is self-centric. Realize that it's all a futile waste of time. Time that could be spent creating beautiful things in the world. Time that could be spent being kind to yourself. Notice that there isn't a higher purpose neither for that suffering nor for your thoughts surrounding it. Notice how unintelligently you react to it all.

Only then will you laugh at yourself. Oh, how many times I nod my head at myself in agreement with how stupid what I was suffering with really was. During meditation, it happens to me a lot.

And this is your freedom from suffering. You get to it from the inside, not from anything or anyone on the outside.

And once you are free, you will know what to do and take the right action toward solving any challenge or problem. Then you can act from a place of vision and greater responsibility toward yourself and the world, not from a place of hurt and suffering that serves nobody.

This is *the* most important thing for you to do. To find peace in your inner world. Then your outer world will start to mirror your inner world. The world is but a reflection of your own inner state or inner conflict.

Here are some signs that may be a good indication that you are becoming more spiritually awake:

- an increased tendency to let things happen rather than make them happen and feel the flow of life

- frequent attacks of giggles and random smiling with or without a reason

- feelings of being connected with others, with nature, and with everything around you

- frequent overwhelming episodes of appreciation and gratitude

- an unmistakable ability to enjoy each moment

- a loss of interest in conflict and an inability to worry much

- a loss of interest in interpreting or interfering in other people's business

- a loss of interest in judging others and yourself

- an incredible ability to love without expecting anything in return

· a loss of interest in owning stuff and the increased desire to purge and have less

· a desire to eat healthier and take better care of your body

· seeing synchronicities in your life and manifesting your desires

We sit down to meditate to seek enlightenment and awareness, but what do we do instead? We fight. A war goes on inside. One between your higher self and you. A conflict between our current thoughts and the thoughts we think we're supposed to have. We fight with our own thoughts. We judge them. And then we wonder why there is so much violence in the world and why nations go to war and innocent people have to die.

Wouldn't people—and life—be much more enjoyable if we could sit with the truth and not battle with who we are? In a moment of jealousy, I am jealous. I don't need to compare, judge, or feel threatened. All I have to do is observe. Observe and let go. Children are especially marvelous at this. They know that sometimes they like a particular toy, and sometimes they don't. Sometimes they want to laugh at something funny, and sometimes they don't. They have no judgment, no attachment, and no war inside. Adults shortchange themselves with the idea of "the perfect self." It blocks them from being their true selves. Our mind is not the problem, nor are our thoughts, not even our conditioning. The problem is the unawareness of that conditioning. Peace is born from the state of comfort with who you are as is. But we need to slow down enough to notice and take our time doing so.

Art students are sometimes required to stand in front of a piece of art and just look at it for two hours. An exercise that is both exhausting and exhilarating. They soon notice how much they originally didn't see and how, for the first time ever, they've seen a piece of art. And if you observe long enough, you will start to notice something so exhilarating —a very important, indisputable fact about life. You will start to notice that in this moment you have all the power in the world to choose your thoughts.

Change your thoughts, and you change your life. At any given moment, you are choosing that one thought you want to focus on. That thought gives you a feeling, and the feeling becomes your experience of this present moment. That thought can be changed. Belief systems from the past have no more power over you than that of this moment when you can change everything. This thought and this moment create your future. You can begin to experience freedom. Total freedom. Right here, right now. Notice the power in knowing this. Be aware.

Exercise

When I offered my program to the group of sixty government officials I mention at the beginning of the book, I prepared a Happiness Kit for each of the participants, and it was such a big hit. It's fun to make and is a beautiful reminder to stay true to our course along this journey to a meaningful life. To create your own kit, you need the following items:

1. A rubber band

2. A star (sticker)

3. A marble

4. A penny

5. An eraser

6. A paper clip

7. A Hershey's Kiss

8. A button

9. A tiny paper bag

The rubber band is to remind you that you can stretch beyond what your mind will say you can. The star is to remind you that that's who you are and you can make a difference. The marble is for the day that you lose yours. There's a penny so that you're never broke and an eraser to remove all the little mistakes—all the little things that you said out of fear instead of love. You have a paper clip to keep it all together. You have a Hershey's Kiss to remember that you're loved, so every time you see a Hershey's Kiss, go get a hug. And there is a button to press in case of panic. Place all these items in the paper bag, and voilà, you have your very own kit.

Chapter 14

Everything Has a Beginning
and an End

The life of clouds is a parting and a meeting.
A tear and a smile.
And so does the spirit become separated from
The greater spirit to move in the world of matter
And pass as a cloud over the mountain of sorrow
And the plains of joy to meet the breeze of death
And return whence it came.
To the ocean of Love and Beauty…to God.

—Khalil Gibran

IT's a truth about life that everything in it arises and ceases. The forever-and-ever concept is misleading. Nothing lasts forever. Everything transforms. Everything has a beginning and an end.

I write this as I watch the Indian Ocean incessantly crash against the reef. It went on all last night and has been going on all day today. It may look like it's the exception, but the more I watch the ocean, the more I notice it is but a series of waves, each arising and ceasing in its own little world and at its own pace. It shows up, does its thing, and then it's gone. And so does one's life. Nothing lasts forever, and we're here to fulfill a role, to birth an idea, to see through a project, to save a life, to make a difference, to be the change, to make this world a better place because we simply listened to our soul and fulfilled its meaningful purpose to serve. That's why we have to live every single moment ever so mindfully, ever so present in it.

When I'm mindfully present, the present moment never ends. The past and the future are but a dream. My visions, thoughts, ideas, and dreams of the future will come through this moment.

Permanence is not found in nature. Everything is impermanent and changing. We assume that we will not change or that we can't, when in reality we are changing all the time with age. We exist in various forms, ever changing as we go through oceans of emotion and experience. We are arising and ceasing all the time.

It's a life of yin and yang and creating balance. It's about having an even keel rather than being like a pendulum. Is it good to eat? How about if we eat all the time? Is it good to fast? All the time? Stay close to a loved one? All the time? Have alone time? All the time? You get where I'm going with this?

Life is not a quest for pleasure, as Sigmund Freud believed. Or a quest for power, as psychotherapist Alfred Adler taught. Life is a quest for meaning.

According to a two-year survey of almost eight thousand students done at Johns Hopkins University, 78 percent said,

"Finding a purpose and meaning to my life," when asked what they considered very important.

Meaning can be found in simple pleasures. So why do people find themselves feeling so empty? It's because of the attitude they take toward their lives, challenges, opportunities, and so on.

The soul is the part of you that tells you to never give up. It's that "I can't put my finger on it" reason to keep going despite all odds. The soul doesn't make exact calculations or plan for how things need to play out. The soul just knows.

Life is difficult. It's not meant to be easy. The sooner we accept that the better off we are because we stop expecting. We stop thinking we are entitled to anything. And then we start living and doing.

Bonnie Ware is an Australian nurse who spent years working in palliative care, tending to patients in the last twelve weeks of their lives. She recorded their dying epiphanies in her blog and later into a book called *The Top Five Regrets of the Dying*. This is what they said:

- "I wish I'd had the courage to live a life true to myself, not the life others expected of me."

- "I wish I hadn't worked so hard."

- "I wish I'd had the courage to express my feelings."

- "I wish I had stayed in touch with my friends."

- "I wish I had let myself be happier."

When you have a clear sense of direction and an unshakeable faith in your strengths and abilities, nothing can stop you from succeeding in all your ventures and having your life be the best road trip ever, without all the regrets. Taking the time to nurture your heart, master your mind, nourish your body, and feed your soul will bring vitality, energy, and richness to your every day. Make this part of your morning habits. Make it a nonnegotiable ritual. And never give up on yourself. Progress happens in its own time; it is happening without a doubt.

For the first four years after a Chinese bamboo tree is planted, all the growth takes place underground. All you can see is a tiny bulb with a little shoot coming out of it. In the fifth year, this tiny bulb grows into an eighty feet high bamboo tree.

What separates those who live exceptional lives from those who don't is the way they use this time we are given, that new batch of twenty-four hours that we get every twenty-four hours. Let's say you take one hour during the weekend to plan and organize your week and set your well-being goals. This simple act is the secret sauce to a life of well-being and happiness. This ensures you have all the ingredients to a delicious, juicy, colorful life.

We are all one story. We all came from the same one breath of life. Aware or not aware of it, we are all one. At one spiritual retreat I attended in India, we were all sitting in a circle, holding hands with our eyes closed and being guided through a meditation where we truly felt the meaning of oneness. Anybody who has attended a religious service or been to a sports game at an arena knows how difficult it is to resist being one with the people around you. The wave you see in audiences and the standing ovations are both ways of wanting connection with others around us. It's contagious.

We are all one big chain of hearts. Connected hearts. When you learn to take care of your own well-being, you influence others around you to do the same. And when you practice love and random acts of kindness—even for strangers—you then pass along the same practice to all those in your circle, who in turn spread it, and the next thing you know, hundreds, if not more, are doing the same. That's the butterfly effect and what inspired the logo for Be You International and the philosophy behind why I do the work I do.

I love the universe just the way it is. I'm part of it and it's a part of me, and therefore, I love myself just the way I am. I love myself for being me. Thank you, God, for giving me the freedom to be me.

Epilogue

How much more time do you think you will need before you are able to say, "I will create no more pain, no more suffering?" How much more pain do you need before you can make that choice? If you think that you need more time, you will get more time — and more pain. Time and pain are inseparable.

——Eckhart Tolle, *The Power of Now: A Guide to Spiritual Enlightenment*

THE longest-running show on our mental Broadway is the way you respond to the question "How will you live your life?" Will you choose the way of doubt and fear, or will you choose love and wisdom? Let's not be our own enemy. Let's not be a hindrance to our own happy life.

I Believe …

… we need more happy people because happy people change the world. I'm here to build a love generation of happy people who are powered by passion.

I Believe …

… happy people are those who bring their ALL to the game of life and utilize all their God given unique set of gifts, talents, personality, and passion. That's the essence of Being You.

I Also Believe That You Have the Power

The power to step up and change your life and change the world around you along the way. You have the power to choose to get out of your comfort zone and do things differently—more passionately—more you.

It doesn't matter that I'm the only certified Passion Test facilitator in UAE or that I'm trained to be a kids' coach. It doesn't matter that I've gone through one of the most rigorous life coaching certification programs in the world or that I have well over 1000 hours of coaching under my belt. It doesn't matter that I'm a certified Strategic Interventionist or that I have ICF's PCC designation along my BA and Master's in interior design and have many letters after my name.

It only matters that I absolutely kick ass—just like yours—into getting your shit out of the way. So that you have more clarity and space, so you know what your passions truly are and then to have a game plan of how to bring more of that into your ~now~ happy life and the world.

Because We Need More Happy People In the World …

Did I mention this already?!

The first thing you pack when you go on a road trip is a map. When I travel to a new place, before I leave my hotel, I make sure I have a map, and I mark on it where the hotel is so I know how to get back no matter how far I wander. We aren't born with maps. We have to create them without being attached to them because those maps will have to constantly be updated and upgraded as we go through life.

My hope is that this book gave you the tools you need to create your own road map to igniting a life full of love, happiness, and meaning. Some people read a book and run with it. They immediately put into practice what they learned, and their lives are all the better for it. God knows how many books I've read and how many were life changing for me. However, there are some people who need more hand holding and to be walked through a process or an experience rather than just simply read a book so they can absorb and retain the lessons better. Well, I also happen to be one of those people as I've mentioned earlier and that's exactly why I offer PASSIONABILITY as an experiential learning event as well as a one-week retreat. At the very end of the book, you can read what past participants of my events and retreats had to say about them. Hope to meet you at a future event. Until then, I wish you more PASSIONABILITY in your life!

Contact Information

To find out more about upcoming events or private coaching, please visit:

`www.beyouinternational.com`

When you visit the website, you'll be able to enroll in our free online courses at Be Youniversity, download free material, read through Randa's blog posts, watch short videos on various self-help topics, subscribe to the newsletter, and shop in the online store.

To ask questions or share insights, breakthroughs, or realizations you've had as you read this book, please email info@beyouinternational.com

About Be You International & Randa El Zein

Be You International

Commitment to personal growth, happiness, empowerment, and social change is what we thrive to instill in our community. Our highly successful "east meets west" approach brings together the modern Western self-help industry teachings and the ancient Eastern philosophies combining them with a strong affinity to the Middle Eastern's unique cultural and societal norms and traditions in order to deliver practical, easy to understand methodologies, workshop events, and products to inspire life-changing transformation.

Be You International is at the forefront of the empowerment industry in Abu Dhabi and aspires to become one of the key providers of life coaching and innovative empowerment education solutions for Abu Dhabi, the U.A.E, and beyond.

Vision & Mission

Be You International is dedicated to inspiring young people to be Powered by Passion™ and to creating empowering services, products and workshops for our community and the world. BYI is committed to inspiring confident future leaders & ambassadors for the greater good and to propagate a message of hope and positivity to the world. Ultimately, BYI intends to be the creator of a new Love Generation and to be of service to it.

Our Logo Philosophy

The butterfly is a symbol of transformation, rebirth, and metamorphosis. Our logo is a butterfly that is formed of little butterflies that come in different colors, shapes, and sizes because we hope to inspire young people who come to us— to embrace their individuality. When we fully become ourselves, utilizing our own strengths and talents doing what we love, that's when we serve the world best. Simply BEing YOU can make such a big difference.

The logo symbolizes the collective effort required to create a more passionate world. We are empowered knowing that our smallest words and actions have the power to start change. The border of our big butterfly is left open to show that the sky is the limit for each of those little butterflies transforming the world in their own time, in their own way, at their own pace. We are all unique in our own be-you-tiful way. We are not born to be confined in a mold and be all the same. Our freedom to be who we are enables us to be the change we want to see in the world. This is the essence of a Love Generation.

What is a Love Generation?

"If you want to go fast, go alone. If you want to go far, go together." – African Proverb

The Love Generation is a revolution—a social movement of happy young people who are powered by passion because they choose to conquer their fears and live their best lives, fulfill their potentials, and follow their passions to change their world. Happy people change the world. But we can't do it alone. This is our collective effort creating the shift needed in this part of the world. Together we can create this Love Generation.

Randa El Zein

Randa is a Canadian citizen who was born in Lebanon and raised in the United Arab Emirates where her dad (her favorite person in the world) had started his own entrepreneurial business since before the UAE was united! She's travelled far and wide for her education in pursuit of her number one passion at the time, interior design. Randa lived in Italy and used it as a home base for travelling throughout Europe, pursuing her other passion for travel.

Randa moved to Canada while in her twenties and lived there for almost a decade. While there a series of life-changing events motivated her to leave her career in interior design and real estate and completely shift gears. She pushed herself hard to become equipped with the necessary tools, certifications and trainings to aid her in the newfound, number one passion of building and being of service to a Love Generation. She made this leap of personal faith because of an actual dream she had while attending a women's retreat. This one dream flipped her life right side up! And her journey began. Randa founded Be You International in Toronto, Canada and shortly after that she moved back to expand into UAE. The bonus was that she was able to be close to her family and make a difference in that part of the world.

Leave A Review: Share The Love

If you've read this far and enjoyed the book, kindly leave a review on Amazon or the platform you used to purchase the book. And then maybe consider passing it along to someone you know would benefit from this book instead of just leaving it sitting on a shelf.

Acknowledgments

MY heart is overflowing with gratitude. My eyes are full of tears. This book would not have been possible without the help of so many. It's so hard to know where to start.

I want to say thank you to Filomena for giving me a most beautiful space to start the writing of this book back in 2012 and for the delicious carrot and ginger energy drinks she made me every morning to keep me going.

I want to thank my editors at Kirkus who literally helped me transform the book into the polished end result you have in your hands, over the course of 6 months of thorough editing.

Thank you to my friends Christina and Judy who read through the advanced manuscript and gave me their feedback and amazing reviews. Thank you to Mitzi for proofreading and making sure our book is as error free as is humanly possible.

I want to also thank Judy for nagging me over the last 4 years or so to finish the book and for kicking my butt whenever I procrastinate.

Thank you to all my clients, family and friends who helped me through the agony of firming up the title of the book, choosing the perfect subtitle and voting for their favorite cover design.

Thank you to Zeljka for hitting the nail on the head with her magic on the cover design, for bringing life into the word PASSIONABILITY and for her patience with my million little editing suggestions. Thank you to Steve for making my book look pretty and professional on the inside and for being patient with my request for more butterflies. Thank you to Jessica for the index and because of admitting how she got distracted from her indexing task because she loved what she was reading, which of course made my day.

Thank you to Zubair and Tin for being the heroes behind the scene doing all the million tasks I'm incapable of doing. Without them, I wouldn't have had the time to write or create.

During the last 2 months of the process of finalizing the book and having it ready to be published, and all the stress that coming with learning how to do something for the very first time, I have to thank Andrea for his amazing support and encouragement. He said going forward I have to finish a book per year and bought me a new Mac fit for the challenge. He melted my heart.

Of course, special thanks go also to my parents. In their own different ways, they helped me to be where I am today. And where I am, is a very beautiful place where I get to walk my talk and live a life ignited with PASSIONABILITY.

Notes

1. *Social Intelligence: The Revolutionary New Science of Human Relationships: Beyond IQ, Beyond Emotional Intelligence*, by Daniel Goleman, page 3

2. *The How of Happiness: A Scientific Approach to Getting the Life You Want, by Sonja Lyubomirsky*

3. *The Outliers: The Story of Success*, by Malcolm Gladwell, page 52

4. *Happy for No Reason: 7 Steps to Being Happy from the Inside Out*, by Marci Shimoff and Carol Kline, page 17

5. *The Happiness Advantage: The Seven Principles of Positive Psychology That Fuel Success and Performance at Work*, by Shawn Achor

6. *The 7 Habits of Highly Effective People: Powerful Lessons in Personal Change*, Stephen R. Covey, page 70

7. *The Village Effect: How Face-to-Face Contact Can Make Us Happier and Healthier*, by Susan Pinker, page 179

8. *The Subtle Art of Not Giving a F*ck: A Counterintuitive Approach to Living a Good Life*, by Mark Manson

9. www.thework.com

10. *The 7 Habits of Highly Effective People: Powerful Lessons in Personal Change*, by Stephen R. Covey

11. *Loving What Is: Four Questions That Can Change Your Life*, by

Byron Katie and Stephen Mitchell

12. *The Forty Rules of Love: A Novel of Rumi* by Elif Shafak, page 257

13. *Thrive: The Third Metric to Redefining Success and Creating a Life of Well-Being, Wisdom, and Wonder*, by Arianna Huffington, both studies mentioned on this page and others related to sleep and meditation are referenced in this book.

14. *Thrive: The Third Metric to Redefining Success and Creating a Life of Well-Being, Wisdom, and Wonder*, by Arianna Huffington

15. *The Outliers: The Story of Success*, by Malcolm Gladwell, pages 3-12

16. *The Leptin Diet: How Fit Is Your Fat?*, by Byron J. Richards, pages 42-50

17. *Social Intelligence: The Revolutionary New Science of Human Relationships: Beyond IQ, Beyond Emotional Intelligence*, by Daniel Goleman

Recommended Reading

Connected: The Surprising Power of Our Social Networks and How They Shape Our Lives: How Your Friends' Friends' Friends Affect Everything You Feel, Think, and Do, by Nicholas A. Christakis and James H. Fowler (New York: Back Bay Books, 2011)

Creativity Rules: Get Ideas Out of Your Head and Into the World, by Tina Seelig (New York: Harper One, 2017)

Daring Greatly: How the Courage to Be Vulnerable Transforms the Way We Live, Love, Parent, and Lead, by Brené Brown (New York: Avery, an imprint of Penguin Random House, 2015)

Happy for No Reason: 7 Steps to Being Happy from the Inside Out, by Marci Shimoff and Carol Kline (New York: Free Press, 2009)

Influence: The Psychology of Persuasion, by Robert B. Cialdini, PhD (New York: Harper Collins, 2007)

Intimate Behavior: A Zoologist's Classic Study of Human Intimacy, by Desmond Morris (New York: Kodansha Globe, 1997)

Loving What Is: Four Questions That Can Change Your Life, by Byron Katie and Stephen Mitchell (New York: Three Rivers Press, 2003)

Man's Search for Meaning, by Viktor E. Frankl (Boston: Beacon Press, 2006)

Me to We: Finding Meaning in a Material World, by Craig Kielburger and Marc Kielburger (Mississauga: John Wiley & Sons Canada, 1982)

Outliers: The Story of Success, by Malcolm Gladwell (New York: Penguin Group 2008)

Social Intelligence: The Revolutionary New Science of Human Relationships: Beyond IQ, Beyond Emotional Intelligence, by Daniel Goleman (New York: Bantam Dell, 2007)

The 8th Habit: From Effectiveness to Greatness, by Stephen R. Covey (New York: Free Press, 2005)

The Dance of Anger: A Woman's Guide to Changing the Patterns of Intimate Relationships, by Harriet Lerner, PhD (New York: Harper Collins Publishers, 2005)

The 5 Love Languages: The Secret to Love That Lasts, by Gary D. Chapman (Chicago: Northfield Publishing, 2010)

The Forty Rules of Love: A Novel of Rumi, by Elif Shafak (Penguin Random House, 2015)

The Four Agreements: A Practical Guide to Personal Freedom (A Toltec Wisdom Book), by Don Miguel Ruiz (San Rafael: Amber-Allen Publishing, 1997)

The Leptin Diet: How Fit Is Your Fat?, by Byron J. Richards (Tucson: Truth in Wellness Books, 2006)

The Passion Test: The Effortless Path to Discovering Your Life Purpose, by Janet Bray Attwood and Chris Attwood (New York: Penguin Group, 2008)

The Power of Now: A Guide to Spiritual Enlightenment, by Eckhart Tolle (London: New World Library, 2005)

The Rational Optimist: How Prosperity Evolves, by Matt Ridley (New York: Harper Collins, 2011)

*The Subtle Art of Not Giving a F*ck: A Counterintuitive Approach to Living a Good Life*, by Mark Manson (New York: Harper Collins, 2016)

The Untethered Soul: The Journey beyond Yourself, by Michael A. Singer (Oakland: New Harbinger Publications and Noetic Books, 2007)

The Village Effect: How Face-to-Face Contact Can Make Us Happier and Healthier, by Susan Pinker (Toronto: Random House Canada, 2014)

Thrive: The Third Metric to Redefining Success and Creating a Life of Well-Being, Wisdom, and Wonder, by Arianna Huffington (New York: Harmony Books, 2014)

You Can Heal Your Life, by Louise L. Hay (Hay House, 2004)

Recommended Experiential Learning Events

The Work of Byron Katie

www.thework.com

The Work is a simple yet powerful process of inquiry that teaches you how to question and transform negative and stressful thoughts. Through their website you can download their free worksheet and do the work.

The Passion Test

www.thepassiontest.com

Janet Bray Attwood and Chris Attwood's Passion Test is the effortless way to discovering your passions. It's the perfect tool to align your life with what you are most passionate about.

Vipassana Meditation

www.dhamma.org

Courses are given in numerous meditation centers and locations around the world. Each location has its own schedule of courses. Refer to the website to find the closest location near you.

Tony Robbins

www.tonyrobbins.com
Tony Robbins is a best-selling author, philanthropist, and the number one life and business strategist in the United States. For more than four decades, more than fifty million people have enjoyed his warmth, humor, and transformational power.

One World Academy

www.oneworldacademy.com
A philosophy and meditation school based in India.

Take the Step Weekend Intensive

www.gracecirocco.com
Grace Cirocco is a best-selling author, gifted coach, intuitive healer, and one of Canada's most passionate speakers.

Kind words about experiential learning workshop events

"I didn't expect this sort of workshop to work for me, although I came with an open mind. It brought a lot of real emotions to the surface, however, and allowed me to take control of my happiness it also allowed my friends to see a side to me that is often hidden and only shown to those I have come to trust over many years. I feel like a burden has lifted and I am ready to make healthier choices for myself. Thank you, Randa. Thank you for giving me the faith that my happiness is my choice." - EJ

"Very inspiring and knowledgeable experience. A definite energy booster for today, tomorrow and the future. Sincere thank you for instilling magical moments & techniques that will help me achieve at least 1, if not all my goals. You are a true inspiration for a great beginning to anyone your life crosses path with. Keep up the wonderful work." - Maha Al Adhami

"An upbeat and engaged event where clarity takes over from confusion and low energy. I thoroughly enjoyed the evening and left with a number of tools to create a clearer path. Be You is a blessing. Randa, you are sent from Heaven." - Nichola HH, Abu Dhabi

"Dear Randa, If you think positive, sound becomes music ... Movement becomes dance ... Smile becomes laughter ... Mind becomes meditation, and life becomes celebration, I think this what we learned from you in the workshop." - Capt. S. Al Hashemi, Abu Dhabi

"I found that I'm on the right path and already doing what I'm passionate about and this workshop event turned my daily 50%/50% "what if" into 100% "I know" this is my passion. I learned that everything I want can be achieved and I'm responsible for my own happiness. Thank you, Randa." - Dr. Hasini

"Stay big and follow the passion without paying attention to the distractions. This was a very amazing workshop. Randa has a very positive energy that does change you spiritually." -Waad

"Good, interesting and personally challenging in the best way possible." - Mike, Abu Dhabi

"True to her word, Randa gave us a life changing experience." - Salma Mohamed

"I enjoyed talking openly and thinking that there might be a different way and that it is ok to choose happiness. Randa is a great facilitator of open conversation with useful strategies." - Caroline Dredge, Abu Dhabi

"The ability to open and not feel judged, realizing that I am responsible for the focus of my thoughts and that what I allow will continue was what I took away from this workshop. I was engaged so much that I didn't want the session to end. I've learned a lot about myself. Randa creates a safe and positive environment where you are able to realize what your issues are and what you need to work through. I love it! Such a positive atmosphere, a safe haven for any woman to be herself and opening up about things that matter. Also, having the chance to be amongst other women from different backgrounds and cultures helps you see that we are all fighting our own battles no matter where we come from, or what we do in life. We are given the chance to learn from one another, face our fears and insecurities, know what the areas of improvements are, and then eventually make that positive change that makes us feel empowered." - Khulood Alsuwaidi, Abu Dhabi

"The Journaling allowed me to find 'answers' that I didn't know existed. Brilliant experience where I felt safe to share my experience and to find out, not just about others, but about myself! Randa has a terrific gift in making you feel comfortable but also challenging you to work on what you want." - Claire Larelle, Abu Dhabi

"Randa's workshops are about challenging tough questions in a very positive environment. You go away with thought provoking affirmation and a more positive idea about yourself and life in general." - Teresa Murphy, Abu Dhabi

"Randa's workshops always rejuvenate and renew my hope and faith in myself, relationships, people and my focus and perspective in life. I learned about the need of truly 'letting go' of what I don't have in my life and embracing the current situation. It was presented extremely well and was very interesting, fun and interactive, a wonderful experience with lessons and ideas to carry throughout my life to create a better happier life." - Anyetta Saldukas, Abu Dhabi

"The lessons were deep and the group was small enough to focus on individual issues. My 'a-ha' moment was be you, be true to yourself. Randa's enthusiasm and knowledge on a wide range of common issues was impressive!" - Aisha, Abu Dhabi

Kind words from students at universities and schools

"Randa El Zein provided a series of dynamic and engaging programs for OPEN DAY 2014 at Paris Sorbonne University Abu Dhabi. I met her briefly at the NAJAH Education Fair in October 2013 and knew immediately that she had a message that I wanted to incorporate into my next Open Day. The presentations were titled Powered by Passion and working with groups of students, she was able to help them explore the where, when, why and how of determining their passion in life. In particular, these presentations focused on empowering the students with the awareness needed to make a university selection decision and we all know that this is a major choice. Each program was met with an enthusiastic audience of young learners and I sincerely believe that on this day we provided them with valuable skills in order to move forward in life." - Angela Franklin, Sorbonne University, Abu Dhabi, UAE

"This workshop couldn't have come at a better time. There are a few things I've been wanting to do but scared to. Randa's energy is infectious. The whole time I was thinking I want to get to a point where I feel like she does. I know I will." - Shushu

"I realised what I really value in my life and to what extent I am hungry for those things. We all know what we want even when we think we don't. Sometimes we need reminding. This workshop was just a nice friendly reminder to set us on the right path and to help us remember how much potential we each hold within, how much beauty and magic we all have!" - Aneesa Rabbani

"This workshop came at the perfect time just as I was tackling my procrastination problem. I had a renewed motivation seeing Randa (another example) living her life with passion which reminds me to stay focused." - Mohamed Hussain

"It was very enjoyable in many ways. Students relate very well, having someone like this can actually make us better people, the enthusiasm was inspiring. Keep it up, people like you change this world." - Leyan Awwad

"We need more people like this in our life, people who support our dreams and help us choose our future, it is one of the best workshops I've ever been to!" - Maria Kahale

"Highly inspirational. I am 100% sure what I want to be in the future but I feel have much better ideas for my future now." - Mariam Othman Elsayed

"I enjoyed how Randa related to what we wanted, the workshop helped me a lot in realising what I want, and this is truly one of the most motivational workshops I have ever attended! I truly recommend it to any of you who aren't sure of what you want to do in life." - Shamma J.J.

"This workshop was very exciting especially it being not a school academics topic. It changed my life and the best part was the meditation and the humor, I felt so inspired and that it related to us so much." - Sarah Alameri, Abu Dhabi Grammar School

"I enjoyed how Randa let us meditate and think deeply about things we should think of at an earlier stage in our lives, especially that we are 12 graders and we need to decide what we're gonna do with our lives soon. This workshop was very effective." - Lubna, Al Rawafed School

"I enjoyed the fact that it made me empowered again, kind of like a rebirth. If there were more workshops like this the world would be a better place, it gives you a better perspective of how to attain potential trapped within you." - Hajer Moumi

"I learned a lot about my passions, and learned how to set priorities when it comes to passions. The play shop was a great experience; I found it extremely useful, and inspirational. I believe it will affect my life from now on and influence every decision I make in the future." - Haneen Al noman, AIS

"Connecting to my heart was the best part. The teen playshop has helped me greatly to clear out the chaos in my head and figure out what my heart was screaming out to me, I also have acquired skills I can use to get back on track in case I lose my way again. I am very grateful for this experience." - Mohammad Maarrawi, AIS